WHEN HE CAN'T

COMMIT

What To Do When You Fall For An Ambivalent

Man

RHONDA FINDLING

When HE Can't Commit: What To Do When You Fall For An Ambivalent Man

was originally published by Adams Media as *The Commitment Cure: What To Do When You*

Fall For An Ambivalent Man

Copyright ©2004, Rhonda Findling

ISBN: 978-1975921347

Also by **Rhonda Findling**

Don't Call That Man! A Survival Guide To Letting Go

Don't Text That Man! A Guide To Self Protective Dating In The Age Of Technology

Don't Lose That Man! How Women Sabotage Their Opportunities For Successful Romantic Relationships And What They Can Do To Change

Men Who Run From Love: How To Have A Relationship With A Relationship Phobic Man

A Teenager's Memoir: Surviving Parental Abandonment in The Revolutionary 70's

Portrait Of My Desire

Table of Contents

Introduction

INTRODUCTION

Have you ever been aggressively pursued by a man who started acting cold and distant after you'd dated a few months? Has a man ever acted enamored by you only to reject you after you'd been brave enough to make the first move? Did you ever spend a passionate weekend with a man who completely disappeared for a month or forever? If you've lived through any of these painful scenarios, then you've encountered an Ambivalent Man.

When people fall in love they always have some mixed feelings about the object of their affection. No one is a 100 percent sure, no matter how smitten he or she is. The type of man I refer to as an Ambivalent Man struggles with a profound sense of confusion that causes him to repeatedly sabotage romantic relationships (or potential romantic relationships) that could have otherwise been healthy and lasting.

The Ambivalent Man always sends double messages. Red light, green light; stop, go; he wants you, he wants to break up; he's into you, he's not into you; he loves me, he loves me not. He can't make up his mind. He's confused, inconsistent, and unpredictable.

On the other hand, the Ambivalent Man also has wonderful qualities, which is why he is often irresistible and so easy to fall in love with. He can be seductive, fun, lovable, helpful, supportive, generous, charismatic, and smart. He also has the capacity to attach and love. Unfortunately it's his attachment and love for you that triggers his powerful ambivalence, causing him to push you away or provoke you into rejecting him.

Ambivalent Men are everywhere. They come in all shapes and sizes. They run the gamut from professionals with Ph.D.s to blue collar workers. Religion, race, and financial status are irrelevant. The one common denominator all Ambivalent Men share is that they are exciting, yet ultimately unavailable.

A perfect example of an Ambivalent Man is Mr. Big from HBO's *Sex and the City.* He's wealthy, sophisticated, handsome, glamorous, sexy, and smooth. Every time he starts to fall in love with Carrie he becomes ambivalent, often provoking a breakup. When they are no longer together and Carrie hooks up with other men, Mr. Big feels safe and starts pursuing her again.

I believe one of the major reasons so many women don't marry is that men are becoming more and more ambivalent about marriage and commitment.

Men seem to be losing whatever manhood it entails to totally commit to a woman they love. Often, Ambivalent Men are terrified of their own feelings, sometimes completely rejecting a woman even if they seem to care about her. Their reluctance to marry is also encouraged by knowing that there are so many women out there who are still so afraid of being without a man that they will compromise their own needs and desires to accommodate a man's ambivalence about commitment.

Even with all the progress women have made in their financial and emotional independence, they still continue to tolerate brutal rejection, chronic abandonment, man-sharing with other women, emotional and financial exploitation, and even outright cruelty, all for the sake of holding onto their man. I've known many women who have sex with a man right after he's broken up with her. They'll exclusively date a man for years even though he's told her he will never marry her. Even if a woman is independent at work and other areas of her life, often she knows no bounds to her slavish, compliant behavior with men.

It's easy for an Ambivalent Man to get away with his ambivalent distancing behavior rather than face his own issues head on when there are so many women out there who are willing to take him on any terms. He never gets to feel the consequences of his ambivalence because there's always an available woman just around the corner. There's no reason for him to change.

I've come to these conclusions about Ambivalent Men from reading thousands of e-mails responding to my books and from interviewing hundreds of men and women who have consulted with me through my private practice. I've also observed this phenomenon culturally and through my own personal social experiences.

In *When HE Can't Commit,* I've devoted six chapters to different prototypes of Ambivalent Men. The Runner, the Man Who Plays Parlor Games, the Casual Dater, the Fling Man, the Eternal Bachelor, and the Ambivalent Cyber Man. You'll often find that their behaviors and symptoms overlap. I will show you how an Ambivalent Man's compulsive need to repeat his dysfunctional past is unfortunately more powerful than his love for you no matter how intense his feelings may seem. I'll also explain how he rationalizes his ambivalent distancing behavior rather than face his emotional issues head on. The insights you gain will help you stop personalizing the Ambivalent Man's relationally destructive and confusing behavior. You'll feel stronger, less hurt, and less rejected by your Ambivalent Man.

You'll learn about the type of Ambivalent Man who is more capable of a committed relationship and marriage. I'll teach you how to know who he is and how to try to create a relationship with him. I also devote a chapter to women who choose to work on relationships with an Ambivalent Man who is more limited in his capacity to love. You'll learn how to connect to him while still maintaining a powerful sense of self and avoiding exploitation.
I'll also explore why you might repetitively fall for Ambivalent Men. You'll find out why you may choose to stay in a relationship with an Ambivalent Man instead of looking for a man who can fully commit to you.

Reading this book will also help you stop feeling needy and desperate when an Ambivalent Man starts to distance. By learning to set boundaries and not buying into his irrational belief system you will stop acting and feeling clingy. You'll learn how to dispute his rationalizations for his ambivalent thoughts and behavior, rather than accepting everything he says at face value. Most important, you'll develop a stronger sense of self and entitlement.

Why am I so sure of my advice? Because I have applied all of these concepts to men and women in my private practice. More than 70 percent of my clients have gotten engaged within two years after working with me. This occurred after they either worked out the relationship with their Ambivalent Man or broke up with him and found someone more emotionally available. I plan to pass the concepts I've shared with my clients on to you.

You can choose to use the information from my book to work on your relationship with your present Ambivalent Man. Or if you decide he is not worth your time and effort you can use your new found wisdom, strength, and sense of entitlement to look for a different type of man who may be capable of a more consistent, emotionally healthier type of love.

ONE

THE RUNNER

Sheila, a forty-year-old attractive administrative assistant, met Dan at a nightclub. He was everything she was searching for. Exactly her age, never married, self-employed, good-looking, charismatic, and a great conversationalist. She was thrilled when he called her the next morning at work and asked her out to dinner. Before she knew it they were seeing each other constantly. Her nights were filled with romantic dinners and passionate lovemaking. On the evening of their second-month anniversary Dan started acting cold and distant. When Sheila confronted him about his behavior Dan said that he was just in a bad mood. After leaving for work the next morning she didn't hear from Dan for days. She left him two messages on his voice mail but he never called back. She tried Dan's work number. His secretary answered and told her he was out to lunch. When he didn't answer the message she left with his secretary,

Sheila realized that Dan had dumped her.

Dan was a classic Runner. Devastated about Dan's sudden and unexplained rejection, Sheila came to see me for a consultation.

Who Is the Runner?

The Runner is an Ambivalent Man who is capable of attachment. He's even able to get into a relationship. The only problem is he can't sustain an ongoing relationship. He always leaves. He's an abandoner.

In a way, he's the worst of the Ambivalent Men because he gets you to start a relationship with him and fall in love with him, only to eventually drop you. He's the ultimate exciting, rejecting lover. When a Runner attempts to become romantically involved with a woman he sabotages the relationship in the following ways:

- He leaves a woman before she has a chance to leave him so he can prevent the trauma of being abandoned again.
- He seduces a woman into loving him only to abandon her, which happened to him as a child. It's   the only way he knows how to relate.

14

- He abandons a woman to rid himself of his own pain from childhood by having her experience what he suffered through.
- He provokes a woman to leave him, setting himself up to repeat the trauma of his childhood.

What Causes His Ambivalent Behavior?

A Runner often had a mother who loved him but was sometimes emotionally unavailable because of her own addictions and other physical or psychological problems. When she was unavailable he felt abandoned, which was painful and traumatizing to him. Having a mother who was inconsistent in her love for her son is the root of the Runner's ambivalence with women. Regardless of his mother's limitations he still loved her tremendously. This is why Runners are often lovable and easy to bond with. They have the capacity to love in a limited way, but they don't have the inner resources to connect with a woman in an enduring, committed fashion. When a Runner meets a woman he's attracted to, he often puts her on a pedestal, just the way he idealized his unavailable mother when he was a boy. The Runner hungers for that ancient love he had when his mother was loving and emotionally available, so he often pursues a woman he's interested in ardently, even if she doesn't reciprocate his interest.

Needing to actively engage his ambivalent mother when she was unavailable, he perfected his abilities to seduce and charm. He re-enacts these behaviors, making a woman feel loved and special when she's the object of his affection. So his adoration in the beginning of a relationship is true and authentic. It's not just an act. It's really coming from a very "young place."

Unfortunately, anyone who is idealized is always eventually dethroned. No one can stay a Goddess forever. Eventually the Runner becomes disappointed in the woman he thought was so wondrous. She can't meet all of his needs all the time. She frustrates him, bores him, has needs of her own, enrages him, isn't picture perfect. She's turned into the mother who always ended up disappointing him. The spell is over.

Runners can't see life and situations in shades of gray. Problems are black and white for them. All or nothing. Loving mother, abandoning mother. He loves you. He loves you not. He can't seem to struggle with his disappointment with the woman while in the relationship, so he feels compelled to flee. He might even try to find another woman in the hopes that she will completely gratify his emotional needs and won't let him down.

Unfortunately Runners aren't aware of their deeper underlying conflicts. That's why they're Runners. They're emotionally disconnected from different parts of themselves. Men who are aware of their emotional problems and conflicts don't flee. They work on issues with the woman they're involved with and, if necessary, go for professional help.

Rather than struggle with their perplexing, overwhelming emotions, Runners make it easier on themselves by building up a case, which I call the "critical list," against the woman. In this mental list, the Runner tells himself everything that's wrong with her. He'll literally convince himself that he shouldn't be with his woman due to all her faults. He'll pick on anything! Her clothes, weight, how much money she earns. Even if he has his own limitations such as joblessness, lack of education, or health or financial problems, he focuses only on the woman's deficiencies, no matter how trivial.

A Runner ultimately talks himself into leaving. Often this critical list is never expressed to the woman, which is why his leaving is so shocking and unforeseen. Sometimes he mysteriously disappears. Other times his exit is dramatic. All he knows is he's got a whole case built up against the woman he loves. He's off the hook. She's the fall guy. He's on the run.

Sheila finally heard from Dan a couple of months later. He called and asked if she'd meet him for a drink. Shelia decided to see him to hear what he had to say. Two Tequila Sunrises later, Sheila asked Dan why he left. He said that he didn't think she was such a good housekeeper and wanted a more domestic girlfriend. He also thought she should exercise more and stop smoking. Sheila asked him why he spent so much time with her since he knew she wasn't a Martha Stewart clone and she'd been smoking since the first night they met. He told her he didn't know why but was sorry and missed her. He realized that leaving her was a mistake and wanted to get back together. She told him she needed some time to think about it.

What Can You Do When He Leaves?

After a Runner disappears, your instinct is to immediately chase after him. Talk some sense into him. Find out why he's hurting you like this. Why he's destroying the relationship, the love and passion you both experienced together, the magical wondrous moments. It may be painful, but there are some definite no-no's that apply to this situation:

- **Don't waste your time trying to get an explanation out of him.** He has no true authentic answer for his confusing behavior except for his critical list which will only hurt you. His abandoning behavior is already traumatizing enough. You don't need to hear his distorted logic that blames you.

- **Don't try to convince him to stay.** He can't hear you now. He's in the throes of compulsively needing to get away from you. Instead, you must take all of your newfound insight into the Runner and muster up every ounce of strength you have to do nothing. Don't chase after him. Pursuing him as he's running from you will only erode your self-esteem. It'll make you look clingy and pathetic. You'll feel humiliated, which will only feed into your desperation.

Even though it may be painful, it's important that you follow these rules:

- **Let him go.** The moment you realize that he's gone, you must let him go no matter how hard it is; o matter how unnatural it feels. You must force yourself even though your heart's not in it.

- **Don't try to reason with him.** Understand that trying to reason with a Runner while he's in the process of running is putting yourself into a self-defeating, demoralizing, groveling position, which is most certain to make him distance further and only fuel his critical list.

This whole process is excruciating hard work because you've bonded with him. He had a lot of good qualities to offer. There was so much passion. You were so compatible. It's almost unimaginable that he would walk away from all this. True, the pain is so difficult to endure but do not keep hanging on and tolerating dysfunctional rejecting from the Runner.

Elaine, another client of mine, couldn't believe it when Carlos told her he wanted to end their relationship. Even though they had been steadily dating for almost a year, he told he "just wanted to be on his own." Feeling as if she couldn't accept his sudden rejection unless she had a more detailed explanation, she refused to leave his car when they got to her house. Worn down by her insistence he finally yelled back, "If you really have to know, I'm just not attracted to you anymore. Is that enough of a reason?"

Elaine was even more devastated now. Demoralized and humiliated that he actually said he wasn't attracted to her, she felt as if she couldn't go on another moment. She called me to make an emergency appointment for a consultation.

Because a Runner's abandonment feels so cruel and emotionally violating, you must start working on gathering your emotional troops immediately. You'll need as many people in your support system as possible.

The way to detach from him is by mourning and grieving the loss of him, even if your instinct knows he may come back. You have to treat his leaving as an ending. It may be a temporary ending, but in your mind it must be considered a permanent ending.

You must use all of your self-discipline not to pursue him. Call everyone in your support system. Keep expressing your feelings (not to him). Cry. Beat up a pillow. Do whatever it takes to not cling to him. Do not waste your energy obsessing about what you could have done to cause him to leave. The only thing you're guilty of is loving him. Unfortunately your love for him will not heal him or bring him back. In fact, it's receiving your love and feeling love for you that's triggering this maddening, destructive, ambivalent behavior.

Will the Runner Return?

Yes. If you don't pursue him, very often the Runner makes a return appearance. When he feels your absence he may start to worry that you might have gone on with your life. Terrified of commitment and intimacy, Runners sometimes return just offering a casual affair or friendship because they're afraid of a real, full, committed relationship.

Do not let him downgrade the relationship you had together! This kind of ambivalent maneuver is insulting and demeaning. You have to be strong now and stick to what you really want and need. This is when you have work on realizing your sense of entitlement to a full relationship. Don't try to fool yourself into believing you'll be happy just being his friend or a casual sex partner. Insist that if he wants to get back together it has to be a relationship or nothing. You will have to work on strengthening your self-discipline to stick to your demands no matter what.

Keep in mind, though, that if you do decide to go back to a relationship with your Runner, the whole drama can possibly repeat itself unless he resolves his emotional problems. Being involved with a Runner is hard work because he usually has a lot of baggage he needs to work through. You have to decide whether an attempt to have an ongoing relationship with him is worth so much of your time and energy.

After working on her feelings about Dan in psychotherapy Sheila decided that he was too undependable. He had hurt her tremendously and she didn't think she could ever trust him again. In addition, Dan didn't have any insight into his problems or even know there was anything wrong with the way he treated her. Sheila decided not to give Dan another chance. She felt very empowered when she told him she wasn't interested in getting together with him again. She was glad that she had not groveled after him when he disappeared, and instead worked on her own healing and process of letting go.

TWO

THE MAN WHO PLAYS PARLOR GAMES

He always seems so interested in you. Asking questions about what's going on in your life. Gazing into your eyes while he speaks. You've even noticed him checking you out on occasion when you were all dressed up. You can almost cut the chemistry between the two of you with a knife.

The only problem is nothing ever materializes from his seductive behavior. The flirting never goes anywhere. He never asks you out on a date. He's frustrating, confusing, maddening. You wonder if your dating instincts are off. No, you're reading his signals right. The problem is you're dealing with an Ambivalent Man Who Plays Parlor Games.

Who Is the Man Who Plays Parlor Games?

The Man Who Plays Parlor Games is all talk and no action. He seems like he's interested in you but can't make it to the first date.

- A male coworker who's always in your office chatting you up. You both sit together at office meetings. Rumors are circulating that the two of you are a couple. He's your office husband.

- A male professional (supervisor, mentor, teacher, or doctor) who takes a particularly strong interest in you. He goes out of his way to help you out. Boundaries are occasionally crossed. You both socialize and flirt in his professional office.

- A platonic male friend who always flirts with you but never asks you out. He's usually not involved with anyone else.

- A male cyberbuddy who's intensively engaging with you on the Internet but never wants to actually meet in person.

In all these situations, the flirtatious bantering never escalates into a true romance. He hints and teases but can't seem to close the deal. Emotionally healthy men don't fuel chemistry that goes nowhere. If they're interested in something more, even if it's illicit, they will initiate some kind of romantic or sexual encounter pretty soon. They don't stay in indefinite limbo like the Man Who Plays Parlor   Games.

Shari, an attractive thirty-two-year-old saleswoman, met Bob at a spiritual healing conference. He was a handsome Reiki healer and tarot card reader. After striking up a conversation, they found they had a lot in common and went out that night to dinner. When they got onto the topic of relationships, Bob disclosed that he didn't want to become physically intimate with a woman because it interfered with his spiritual work. He explained that relationships were very time-consuming and that he wanted his work to take complete priority in his life. Despite his celibacy, Shari couldn't help but notice that he was dressed very seductively in tight jeans and a sexy shirt with the top buttons undone. His muscular chest was proudly displayed. During dinner he seemed enamored with Shari, asking her personal questions while gazing deeply into her eyes. Shari felt very attracted to Bob and was thrilled when he started calling her after the conference. When they spoke on the phone Bob often called Shari "baby" as if she were his girlfriend or lover. When she mentioned getting together in person, he always came up with an explanation as to why he couldn't meet up with her. Bob was an Ambivalent Man sending Shari double messages.

What Causes His Ambivalent Behavior?

The Man Who Plays Parlor Games probably grew up with a mother who was cold, distant, and rejecting—maybe even contemptuous toward him. There's a chance he was emotionally and/or physically abused as a child. Loving someone only brings up feelings of betrayal and pain in him. He feels more comfortable and less anxious keeping a firm boundary, almost like a fortress.

However, being only human, he also craves intimacy despite his fears. So he handles his simultaneous anxiety and longing for closeness by manipulating a woman into experiencing *his* feelings. This process is known as projection.

Projection means attributing one's feelings, thoughts, and fantasies onto another person, because feeling these things for oneself is uncomfortable and/or causes anxiety. So when a Man Who Plays Parlor Games acts seductive and flirtatious with you, and you get turned on by his attention, that is what he feels for you. He has gotten you to struggle with the same feelings he's trying not to deal with. He doesn't act on the messages he's sending you with his behavior because he's often not in touch with his own feelings (which is why he projected them onto you!). He's confusing and makes you feel as if he's playing games.

During the course of their phone discussions Shari found out that Bob was sexually abused as a child. It appeared he had difficulty struggling with his conflicts about his sexual longings because they triggered traumatizing memories. As a result he acted out his sexual urges that he was trying not to feel by dressing seductively and calling Shari "baby." He managed to get Shari to feel desire for him, which is what he was originally feeling for her and trying to rid himself of. Now she's struggling with his projected feelings, and her own feelings of desire and frustration that the friendship isn't really going anywhere romantically.

Why Does He Act This Way?

Here are the *real* reasons why some men play Parlor Games:

1. **He is terrified of closeness.** While a Runner has the capacity to attach but can't sustain a relationship, an Man Who Plays Parlor Games can't even reach that level of intimacy. He is usually single and unattached because he's terrified of risking closeness for even a little while. He's in an awful

predicament because he craves closeness and pushes it away at the same time. His ambivalence about intimacy causes him to send you mixed signals.

2.   **He is struggling with sexual identity issues.** He may be in the process of coming out of the closet. He's trying to have a relationship with a woman, but his heart really isn't in it. Deep down he's really attracted to men but not ready to face his reality, thus the mixed messages. There are also Men Who Play Parlor Games who are ashamed of their sexuality. They long for a woman but are afraid of expressing their sexual interest. These men may be struggling with sexual dysfunction such as premature ejaculation or impotency.

3.   **He is contemptuous toward women.** The most dangerous type are man is the one who gets pleasure from teasing women with a relationship knowing he's never going to ask them out. This kind of ambivalence might result from a childhood with an abusive or overly seductive mother. He most likely felt powerless growing up. He acts out now by making you feel helpless, frustrated, and rejected the way he might have felt as a boy or adolescent.

4.   **He is involved with another woman.** Some men are truly interested in a woman they're acting seductive with, but are already involved

with someone else. This type of man is not usually suffering from a traumatic childhood. He is authentically confused about whether he should pursue a relationship with a woman due to prior commitments. Unfortunately the thrills and chills of the seductive encounter is often the end of the road. Unless he leaves the woman he's already involved with, this situation can be very disappointing and frustrating for someone who is highly interested in this man.

The common thread that all Men Who Play Parlor Games share is that they are not open and honest about their feelings, which causes a woman to become confused and frustrated. Due to his lack of connection between his behavior, his thoughts, and his emotions, this type of Ambivalent Man is indeed very confusing.

How to Handle a Man Who Plays Parlor Games:

You can protect yourself from getting hurt by a Man Who Plays Parlor Games in many ways. Read through the list below to learn how to handle his ambivalent behavior and make yourself less vulnerable.

- **Don't Invent a Relationship**

Once you've determined your man is playing Parlor Games, you must try not to read so much into what he says to you. Always remember that action speaks louder than words. Unless a man can act on his flirtation, don't let his verbal stuff carry a lot of weight.

It's essential that you protect yourself by not putting too much emotional energy into a man you're not dating or having an affair with. You have to keep the limitations of this connection in perspective. Until you've gone out on a romantic date or been in a sexual physical encounter with him, it's still strictly platonic or professional no matter how seductive he is. The bottom line is, don't invent a relationship. If you do, you'll be setting yourself up for deep disappointment and heartbreak.

Vanessa met Alan on the Internet in a chat room. Living in different parts of the country, they began sending each other long intimate e-mail letters. They spoke on the phone on only two occasions. Vanessa thought about Alan all the time and thought she had finally met the man of her dreams. She denied the fact that he never gave her his home phone number and rarely answered his cell phone. She began referring to Alan as her boyfriend when she spoke to her friends about him. To Vanessa's shock and dismay he completely disappeared after two months. When he finally contacted her, he confessed he was married and had gone back to his wife. Although Vanessa had enjoyed her brief connection with Alan, she realized this was not a real relationship, but an invented one.

- **Don't Idealize Him**

See him as he really is. Don't put him on a pedestal and worship him. Don't delude yourself. Even if he's brilliant, understanding, charismatic, funny, warm, successful, and famous, there's something not right about him. Idealizing a man is a powerful coverup for negative feelings that you're afraid of facing. To facilitate working through your idealization, get in touch with your negative feelings about him. Anger and rage for instance. Aren't you the least bit insulted that he doesn't want to date you or become sexually involved? What about your feelings of frustration? Confusion? Aren't you angry that he may be wasting your time? Being in touch with all of your feelings including uncomfortable ones will empower you to resolve this situation and make healthier choices.

Emily was working at her new job as a receptionist for a week when Tony, an exceptionally handsome senior advertising executive, started flirting with her. Despite his daily seductive behavior he never initiated getting together outside of work. Tired of waiting for him to make the first move, Emily asked Tony out to lunch. He turned her down explaining he was busy. Despite her disappointment Emily can't stop thinking about how handsome and charismatic he is. When she goes out on dates with men who are interested in her, Emily compares them to Tony. Idealizing Tony is preventing Emily from developing a real relationship with a man who is available and not playing Parlor Games.

- **Don't Stay in the Situation**

What's keeping you hooked on a man who can't get it together to date you or even have an affair? Are you hoping against hope that he'll come through for you? Try looking deeper. Is he a substitute for a real relationship? Are you too lazy or too anxious to pursue a man who can offer you more? Do you have a need for some kind of drama to fill the emptiness of your life? Are you attached to painful, frustrating situations? Why are you willing to settle for so little? Why don't you think you're entitled to more?

Okay, may be he's bringing some positive aspects into your life. He's paying attention to you, offering support, helping your career, giving you advice, and bringing some excitement into your life. Keep in mind, though, that being involved with a man who does not want a romantic relationship or even an affair can reek havoc on your self-esteem. He can make you feel unattractive, unwanted, unloved, deprived. Being attracted to someone who's continually frustrating and rejecting you is humiliating and self-defeating. So, if you want to feel better about yourself, he's not going to help you; in fact, he'll make you feel worse.

- **Pulling the Plug**

After much contemplation you've decided not to tolerate Parlor Games anymore. So what now? Set a limit. Make a decision on how much time you'll give for the relationship to switch into the romantic dating mode. Otherwise, you could passively wait around, letting his ambivalence take over your life. When your time limit is up, you can take the following steps to be more proactive:

Make the first move. If you want to find out once and for all if he has any capacity for taking this connection to another level, make the first move yourself. Ask him to go out for a drink, coffee, or lunch. If he turns you down or backs out of the date, then you know nothing is ever going to happen with him. He's wasting your time and definitely playing Parlor Games. At least now you know.

Confront him. Another way of cutting to the chase is confronting him about his flirtatious, seductive behavior. However, you're taking a chance he may deny his feelings or actions. If he projects his feelings onto you, cling voraciously to your truth and reality. Don't buy into his denial. Put it back on him. Don't let him humiliate you. Stand by your guns and tell him your impression of his seductive behavior whether he's aware of it or not. *Warning:* This discussion could lead to feelings of rejection and anger for either or both of you. The entire relationship could spoil and even end. So be careful with this decision. The good thing is that you'll be putting the truth out there, which will end the Parlor Games, and he could fess up to his feelings of attraction for you. The best part is you'll no longer be in limbo.

Just end it. If you don't want to risk the chance of rejection, and you want to get out of limbo and your state of anxiety, then just end it. Consider the whole connection with him a washout, and detach without even telling him why.

Detaching from the Man Who Plays Parlor Games

You've tried everything you can to get him to come around, but he's still playing games. It's definitely time to walk away. The following tips should help you as you move onward and upward:

- **Create physical distance.** Don't leave your door open at the job, switch doctors, drop your class, change your circle of friends for a little while, change your coffee shop, bars, nightclubs, and so on.

- **Stop participating in his seductive dance.** Remember it takes two to play Parlor Games and who knows? Maybe distancing is the one thing he needs to finally bring him to his senses about how important you are to him.

- **Allow yourself to grieve.** Letting him go will be a loss for you because you had a connection with him. You had a fantasy of a future together, which you'll have to mourn now. You may find that it won't be as painful as you imagined because he never really was your boyfriend or lover. That's the one beneficial part of the connection never having amounted to anything.

Rose, an aspiring novelist, was in a writer's group led by Stanley, a published writing teacher whom she greatly admired. She noticed that Stanley paid more attention to her than anyone else in the group, which made Rose feel special. One evening the group went out to a bar for a drink and Stan sat down right next to Rose in a booth. He gazed deeply into her eyes and kept touching her arm when he spoke. At the end of the night he hugged her goodbye, which he didn't do with anyone else. Rose was very attracted to Stanley at this point and was hoping he'd ask her out on a date. When she went back to the writer's group it was business as usual. He acted as if nothing happened that night at the bar.

Rose came to consult with me at this time due to her ongoing frustration and disappointment with Stanley. She discussed her difficulty coping with her crush on Stanley, along with the double messages he was sending her. Because she was very sensitive to rejection, she decided that she didn't want to risk confronting Stanley or initiating a date. The whole situation was beginning to interfere with her writing and everyday life, so after much contemplation Rose decided that it was in her best interest to leave the group. She thought that if Stanley was really interested in dating her, he had her phone number and could just call her up and ask her out.

Although Rose never did hear from Stanley again, she felt much better not having to deal with his ambivalence anymore. Freed from her frustration and anxiety about Stanley, she was able to concentrate on her novel, which she quickly completed.

Rose and other women I've treated have sworn that after dealing with men who play Parlor Games, they will never let themselves get caught up in a man who's all talk and no action ever again!

THREE

THE CASUAL DATER

Sue met Ken, a commodities trader, at a gathering at her friend's house. Although he was okay-looking, she wasn't that crazy about him. He seemed like nice guy, but the chemistry level wasn't very high. When he asked her to go to a Broadway play, Sue decided to give him a chance. To her surprise, they had a good time. Afterward, he called her every Wednesday and asked her out for the following Saturday night. He always took her to glamorous yet elegant restaurants. She was sure he was seriously interested in her, figuring no man would go to these lengths for just a fling. Soon he was asking her out for both Friday and Saturday nights. It appeared their dating was leading to a relationship so she decided to take the emotional risk and become sexually involved with Ken. On the tenth date Ken told Sue that he didn't see them "having a future together" and "thought they should stop dating." He explained that he "wanted to get married but didn't want to marry her." Sue was devastated and shocked because she didn't really like Ken so much in the beginning and had tried to be mature about it and give him a chance. How could she have been so wrong about him and let herself get hurt like this? Unfortunately, she had run into a Casual Dater.

Who Is the Casual Dater?

Don't set yourself up for disappointment! Below is a list of signs that you're seeing a Casual Dater. If your guy is exhibiting these signs, he may not be able to go beyond a few dates before he calls it quits.

- He is a man who is actually looking for a relationship. He really longs for marriage and feels bad that he can't seem to achieve this goal.

- He is reliable and usually makes a good first impression. You can take him anywhere, to Christmas parties, weddings, and family gatherings. In fact, his excellent social skills are honed from dating so often.

- He appears to be capable of a relationship because he really is interested in going out to places rather than just having a fling. He keeps calling you for dates so you think he's very interested in you.

Ironically, many women keep dating the Casual Dater even when they're not that crazy about him, because he gives the impression that he's serious about a relationship and possibly marriage.

What Causes His Ambivalent Behavior?

The main problem with the Casual Dater is that he feels *entitled* to "perfect" women. Despite the Casual Dater's longing for love and relationship, he's deeply committed to being with the kind of women he feels entitled to. He'd rather remain single than be with a woman who doesn't meet his expectations. The irony and maddening part is, he's unable to see his own shortcomings. Even if he's broke, unattractive, or disabled, if a woman doesn't measure up to his ideal he will not want to have a relationship with her.

Some Casual Daters have completely unrealistic expectations of the woman they'd like to have as a girlfriend or wife. They actually compare potential girlfriends to playboy models, movie stars, and fantasy women.

41

They often have crushes on women who are in their lives but are unattainable. Sometimes they date more than one woman at a time. This increases the chances of meeting the perfect woman.

When a Casual Dater finds a woman who meets his expectations, he eventually finds something wrong with her. In other words, he always ends up *devaluing* the woman no matter how great he originally thought she was and how close she was to his ideal. He then becomes ambivalent and either sabotages the potential relationship by giving women the "distancing lecture" or never wanting to go beyond casual dating.

The Casual Dater is superficial and isn't capable of loving on a mature level. He can't accept another human being for who she is, flaws and all, which is necessary in order to have a long-term relationship or marriage. If the woman is going through a personal problem while dating, he has a hard time dealing with it. Although he has a nice demeanor he's basically self-absorbed.

The Distancing Lecture

After he has gone through the process of devaluing you in his mind, he delivers a lecture with one of the following themes:

- "There's not going to be a   relationship."

- "I don't see a future for us."

- "You're a great lady, but I just can't seem to fall in love with you."

- "I want to get married but I don't want to marry you."

The Casual Dater can be very wounding in his need to get rid of you. He's not like the Runner, who just disappears. He will tell you bluntly when it's over. It's therefore important to understand where his lecture is coming from and not take it too personally, although this is easier said than done. Dora met Paul at a lecture on nutrition at an adult learning center. From their discussions, Dora learned that Paul was struggling with chronic fatigue syndrome. He came from a family of great wealth so he was able to support himself despite his physical limitations. He dated a lot, but never had a long-term relationship with a woman. Although she was concerned about his physical disabilities, he seemed like a nice guy and she was on a serious search for a boyfriend. They went on a few dates. When Dora didn't hear from him, she worried that Paul's health had gotten worse, so she gave him a call. Paul told Dora that he didn't know if he wanted to have a relationship with her and was now dating someone else. Stunned, she tried to talk to him about his decision because she didn't understand. Then he had the audacity to tell her he needed to decide if he even wanted to see her again!

Why Does He Act This Way?

Here are the *real* reasons men are Casual Daters:

1.   **He may have had a mother who was emotionally or physically unavailable.** The sad thing is that he didn't develop the inner resources it takes to have a deep enduring relationship because of this mother's unavailability. Instead, he compensated for his lack of nurturing by constructing an ideal vision of a woman who would meet all his needs. It is this perfect woman that he's always searching for.

2.   **He is not in touch with his anxiety about closeness so he blames the woman's flaws for the demise of the potential relationship.** He rids himself of his anxiety about closeness by either rejecting an available woman or never going beyond casual dating. With either solution he never has to deal with his feelings a relationship brings up for him.

3.   **He is unable to look at his own limitations or imperfections.** If he had the insight to understand these dynamics he wouldn't act out his

44

ambivalence by ending a potential relationship or staying in a go-nowhere relationship.

So how can you tell if you're seeing a Casual Dater? The following tips will help to clue you in.

Signs You Are Seeing a Casual Dater

Your Casual Dater can commit more than the Man Who Plays Parlor Games, but ultimately gives himself away as an Ambivalent Man by his inability to take it to the next level.

He's had few or no relationships with women. Although he dates a lot, a relationship never seems to materialize.

- He's a big expert on how to meet new women. He goes to endless singles events, clubs, and dating services to keep up an ongoing search for his ideal woman. Casual Daters are often on the Internet meeting women in chat rooms and online dating sites.

- He uses personal ads a lot. He puts personal ads in newspapers, magazines, and online sites, and responds to women's ads. When he meets a woman on a blind date, he's often disappointed because she's not who he was fantasizing she'd be. His level of attractiveness is irrelevant; only his expectations matter to him.

- He displays a lack of experience in relationships. Sometimes he seems naive when he talks about relationships in general.

- He has tons of dating experience and stories. Sometimes he dates more than one woman at a time. He figures it's a numbers game to find his perfect woman.

- Dating him never escalates to a relationship. He always wants to date around once a week or less. He doesn't show signs that he wants to become more serious. He doesn't want to see you on the holidays or introduce you to his family or friends.

Sherry met Sam after he answered her personal ad online. Just from their e-mail and phone conversations she could tell he was a walking encyclopedia on meeting new women. He seemed to know all the singles events going on around the city. He'd entertain her on the phone for hours with stories of his dating experiences. He rarely mentioned anything about serious long-term relationships. He told Sherry he thought they had a very special connection just from their phone conversations and he was dying to meet her. Due to her hectic work schedule, she didn't have much time. Sam was willing to accommodate her, however, so Sherry decided to take a chance on the day of their meeting. Excited at the prospect of meeting this man who seemed so interested in her, Sherry got all dolled up. When he walked into the restaurant he looked disappointed when he realized it was Sherry. They talked but he left shortly. Sherry didn't think Sam was so great anyway, but she would have been willing to give him a chance. She never heard from him again, but she saw his ad on all the personal ad sites for years after that.

How to Handle the Casual Dater

When responding to his distancing lecture . . .

- **Don't fall apart in front of him!** It's not going to do any good and will make you feel even worse. Freak out when you get home or call your girlfriends, but don't show how you feel in front of him. Don't make a dramatic scene. It's not good for your self-esteem and will not help the situation.

- **Don't feed into his devaluing process by defending yourself.** You are fine the way you are. It's his perception and not necessarily reality

- **Don't, under any circumstances, try to talk him out of his decision.** Show him you have high self-esteem now and don't need his approval. Put all of your energy into staying emotionally grounded.

- **Don't cling to him or grovel.** It is demeaning to you to let a man with severe intimacy problems see that he has such a powerful effect on you. If you grovel, you will regret it later on.

The Casual Dater is into his compulsive need to rid himself of you, which could be pretty compelling, so just go along with it even if it's difficult. Mourn the loss of him, even if it's temporary. Unless he goes for psychological help he may be hopeless. Most important, try not to personalize it. Once again, it's more about him than you, or else his behavior would make more sense. So focus on healing you, and distance from him now.

When you sense he only wants to date and he shows no signs that it's leading to a relationship, there are several actions you can take to change the situation or move on.

Set Limits

Decide how long you're willing to date him without things escalating. Let him know what you want in terms of a relationship. Take a look at the following list of signs that indicate he's willing to take the next step. If your "personal" time limit has come and gone and you still haven't seen any of these signs, it's time to move on.

These are signs that casual dating is escalating toward a relationship:

- He increases the amount of time you see each other.

- He calls more during the week.

- He introduces you to his friends.

- He introduces you to his family.

- He plans a vacation with you.

Confront Him

Find out what his intentions are and what he sees happening in the future with the two of you. This will take courage because you don't know what he'll come back with, but at least you'll know where you stand once and for all. You won't be struggling with his ambivalence. If he gives you a rejecting answer, respond as you would to his distancing lecture, which I covered earlier. It's all one and the same.

Keep It to Yourself

Don't share with him the limits that you set in your own mind. If you don't want to take a chance with a confrontation because you feel you might get hurt or it's too risky, then keep the limits to yourself but act on them just the same.

Think Carefully

Before any confrontation or limit setting you need to put some serious thinking into . . .

- What you want from a   relationship with him.

- What you want from a relationship in general.

- How much time and energy you're willing to emotionally invest in him.

Consider Your Own Needs

Sometimes the Casual Dater won't come around, even if you confront him directly after his distancing lecture. At that point, you need to think about your own:

Ask yourself why you want to be with a man who says he doesn't even know if he wants a future or a relationship with you. Agreeing to see him on his terms makes you look desperate. If you're so emotionally available, you're acting like someone who doesn't deserve to have a man who wants a relationship or future.

If he says he going to work on his issues, your only alternative is to gamble a little time to see if he's true to his word and can conquer his anxiety about relationships. Without psychological help, I don't believe there's much hope. However, if this is the route you want to take, then decide how much time you want to invest in this Ambivalent Man, and honor your time limit.

51

If you decide to keep dating him (with the understanding that there's going to be no relationship or future) your self-esteem will erode and his ambivalent behavior will make you feel like you're going crazy.

If you don't set limits you are enabling him to keep acting out his issues about intimacy. And you, in turn, are acting out your own avoidance of relationships or getting close by being with a man who may not have the capacity for a relationship.

Maria and Marcus were social workers who were introduced at a conference by coworkers. At first, Bob was very enthusiastic about dating Maria, but she was concerned that he had very few relationships in his past and had heard he could be a bit of a playboy. After seeing a number of men who just wanted flings, Maria was hopeful that Marcus and her romance would turn into a relationship with a future. She enjoyed dating him because he took her to concerts and museums, which they both seemed to have a mutual interest in. Suddenly Bob started distancing. First he told her he was going to family functions over the Christmas holiday, and didn't invite her. The next evening when they were watching a video Bob announced that he was still dating other women. He explained that he had been crazy about his ex-college girlfriend who had been cold to him, and could not see himself falling in love with Maria. Crushed and insulted Maria walked out. A week later, Bob called and said that he thought he made the wrong decision and realized he had severe relationships issues he needed to work on. He announced that he was going back to psychotherapy and asked Maria to give him another chance. Maria decided that Bob was worth the risk, especially since he was acknowledging his problems and seeing a therapist. He was also very thoughtful and loving to her while they were dating. She decided she would give him three months to decide if he wanted more with her than just dating. When they ran into trouble again after a couple of months, they went to a couple's counselor his therapist recommended. A year later they got married.

As you can see from what happen with Maria, some Ambivalent Men do have the capacity to work on themselves and have a relationship even if they start out as Casual Daters. In later chapters, you will learn more about Ambivalent Men who have possibilities.

FOUR

THE FLING MAN

Making love to him is electrifying. He looks longingly into your eyes searching your soul. Sometimes he even tells you that he loves you. There's nothing like it. Then two weeks pass before you even hear from him again! No explanation. Just a brief excuse and the seduction starts again. He tells you how much he misses you. He explains he's been very busy but he was thinking of you. At first you resist him but you feel that intense connection kicking in again from just hearing his voice. Your longing takes over and you let him come by. You stay up all night talking and laughing, and of course the sex is fantastic. He takes you out the next morning for a breakfast feast. This time you spend the afternoon together shopping and going to an afternoon matinee. He leaves that night but he doesn't say anything about when he'll see you again. You don't want to ruin things by putting pressure on him. You wait for his call knowing that with all that great bonding you'll probably hear from him by tomorrow. Tomorrow comes but no phone call. Or the next day. No word for two and a half weeks when suddenly you get a message from him on your answering machine. He apologizes for being busy but misses you and wants to get together. Watch out. You're having an encounter with a Fling Man.

Twelve Signs of a Fling Man

So there is no doubt in your mind about who you are dealing with, here are twelve signs of the Fling Man. He may not have them all, but chances are he's got most of them. He's . . .

- Impulsive
- Charming
- A great conversationalist
- Very engaging
- Seductive
- A good listener
- Good in bed

- Usually exhibits some major psychological flaw

- Very sexually experienced

- Mysterious and secretive

- Superficially warm

- Outgoing

Janet met Fred at a nightclub. He was glamorous, sexy, and a great dancer. Although one-night stands weren't her thing, she was so taken with Fred she invited him back to her apartment at the end of the night. The sex was beyond anything she ever imagined. It was just like in the movies. The next morning they went to the local diner and talked for hours over Belgian waffles and endless cups of coffee.

Exhilarated, she told all her girlfriends about him. When a week rolled by and she didn't hear from him, Janet was so disappointed she could barely work. She started to resign herself to the fact that it was a one-night stand. When Fred called her late Tuesday night right before she was about to go to bed, he invited himself over, explaining that he had been so busy with work he didn't have a chance to call anyone. Janet decided to risk seeing him again. They shared another magical night of passionate lovemaking and great conversation. When he left the next morning he said he'd call her in a couple of days. Once again she didn't hear from him. This time he had given her his phone number so she called him. She could tell it was just voice mail, which made her leery. Janet left a message anyway.

A few days later he called her back. Once again he didn't mention going out on the weekend but wanted to get together that night. Unable to resist him Janet let him come over. Right before they fell asleep Fred told her it was the most incredible sex he ever had. When she didn't hear from him again she didn't understand. If he claimed the sex was so great, wouldn't he come back for more? Frustrated and humiliated, she came to see me for a consultation. I explained that Fred was a bona fide Fling Man.

What's a Fling Man?

A Fling Man is a guy who intensely engages with you for a night, afternoon, or weekend, and then totally disappears. He returns out of the blue to have another transcendental experience of emotional and sexual merging of the body and mind.

Having an encounter with a Fling Man is always filled with intense connection. Not just sex, but good conversation and fun as well. It really feels like you're bonding, almost if you were soul mates. You can't imagine this is just a fling; he's got to want more. Sometimes he even tells you he's never felt like this before, even that he loves you.

His ambivalence gets played out when you realize that the magical encounters never materialize into a relationship. Unlike the Casual Dater there is no structure or formalized dating, and unlike the Runner there is no real relationship he's running from. Bottom line is, he's just having a fling. He enjoys the connection until the next time whenever he's in the mood, and you're his flavor of the week, month, or year.

What Makes the Fling Man So Exciting?

A Fling Man knows how to arouse excitement in women. He identifies and caters to their vulnerabilities. He cultivated this personality trait when he was a boy and needed to figure out what his mother wanted to get her love, approval, and attention. Honing these qualities, he knows how to handle women and make them feel special when they're in his presence. Here's what makes him irresistible:

He's great to hang out with because he has the ability to create fun and physical pleasure. He has charismatic charm and the skill of persuasion. He's got a great gift of gab, and when he needs to be, he's a good listener.

He's unpredictable and certainly not boring. You never know when he'll pop up or what he'll do next. Because he is mysterious and elusive, it's easy to project your romantic fantasies onto him and idealize him.

He engages intensely, making you feel adored and desired. When you're with him it seems as if he cares and that you're really in a meaningful relationship, even if it's just for one night or weekend.

Mary met Tom at the Laundromat while they were standing next to each other folding towels. When they got together a couple of times Mary found that she enjoyed his company because he really paid attention to her. He gave her advice on some problems she was confronting with coworkers. He was also a caring and gentle lover, a trait she liked in a man. But their get-togethers were few and far between. He never asked her out in advance but only wanted to get together spontaneously. He was vague about the work he did and how he spent his time. She was shocked when Tom got arrested for insider trading in the stock market. She was embarrassed to admit it, but she was relieved to know that his elusive, mysterious behavior had obviously more to do with his illegal life than it had to do with her.

What's the Real Deal with the Fling Man?

The flip side of the exciting Fling Man is that he will always ultimately disappoint you. He's unreliable and often deceitful. He has a hard time dealing with demands and boundaries. If you ask him what he's been up to while he's not with you he's likely to be defensive, elusive, or lie. The Fling Man's major ambivalence is his intense positive and negative feelings for women. He really is completely into you when you're together. That's why he's so passionate and good in bed. Ironically, great sex actually scares him. He feels enmeshed and engulfed by you. He longs for that transcendent merging feeling as much as you do but is terrified of losing a sense of himself. That's why he distances and disappears after such an intense encounter. But he usually returns when his anxiety about closeness has dissipated.

Because he's not in a real relationship with you, the Fling Man idealizes you when he's with you (just like you idealize him). He projects his fantasy of who he wants you to be. If he took the time to really know you, he'd have to deal with the frustrations and disappointments that occur when people have real relationships. If you make an occasional demand on him, which happens when people start to have relationships, you may not see him around anymore. But if you don't make demands, everything will be on his terms. With the Fling Man, it's hard to express your needs without a consequence, which makes him almost impossible to have a relationship with.

Helen met Harry through a dating service. Harry told Helen that he had never met anyone as wonderful as Helen and that she had all the qualities he was looking for in a woman. This confused Helen since he wanted to get together with her only once in awhile, even though they knew each other three months. Trying to find out more about him, Helen bluntly asked Harry how he spent his time when he wasn't with her. He said that he was a private man and didn't like to discuss his personal business. Hurt by his rejection, Helen decided not to ask him any more personal questions, which prevented their intimacy from deepening.

How Did He Get Like This?

Like the Runner, when the Fling Man distances himself, he's dissociating from you and any feelings he's developed for you. That's one of the main reasons you don't hear from him. He cuts you off in his mind as if you don't exist, so he doesn't have to struggle with his feelings of neediness and dependency that your great encounter brings up for him. Unfortunately some Fling Men do go off with other women as a way of dissociating. Other Fling Men just do their own thing—overwork, go out with their buddies, stay home watching sports, overeat, work out for hours at the gym, get involved in making fast money schemes, gamble, get involved in illegal activities, do drugs or drink, go clubbing looking for more women, and on and on. You won't know what he does with his time unless you ask him, which doesn't guarantee you'll get a straight honest answer.

The reason he hates his needy feelings is a result of his childhood. He probably had an exciting and frustrating, ambivalent mother against whom he is harboring anger and resentment. His mother may have been there for him, loving and close, and then withholding and rejecting. She may have had psychological problems, a physical disability, a dysfunctional relationship with a man, drug addiction problems, or was just exhausted from a stressful life.

As a grown man, the Fling Man is re-enacting with women what was done to him. He excites you with the hopes of things to come—a relationship, like a carrot at the end of a stick—only to abandon you. This way you get to feel the issues he's been harboring and trying to run away from ever since his childhood. If he were more in touch with these feelings he wouldn't need to act them out with you.

A Fling Man projects his neediness onto you by making *you* needy for him by distancing himself from you. He is emotionally and sexually greedy. When he calls you out of the blue, what he wants is to get his emotional and sexual needs met. Then he projects his greediness onto you by believing that *you* are greedy and trying to take away his freedom, because you make demands or want a normal relationship.

The Fling Man is psychologically in worse shape than the Runner because the Runner is capable of a relationship, at least for a limited amount of time. The Fling Man is not capable of even a temporary relationship. He doesn't have the capacity to sustain a deep personal, sexual involvement and permanent love. And because there are so many women out there who are willing to accept him on his terms (at least temporarily), he can manage to get his sexual and some emotional needs met without having to change or work on himself. After his arrest for insider trading, Tom got together with Mary again over drinks at a local pub, and got into a deep discussion. Tom confided that he was taken away from his mother when he was two, because she was suffering from a severe case of bipolar disorder and was unable to take care of him. He remembered that she would hug him a lot, but then would disappear all night long. She apparently used to go out to bars to meet men and even took them home with her. Tom also shared that he'd tried being married a couple of times but the marriages were all short-lived. He now suspected his inability to truly commit to a woman was due to the early trauma of the loss of his mother.

Dealing with the Fling Man

Engulfing him with love and understanding doesn't work with the Fling Man. You need to stand up to him or he will walk all over you, making you an object of his gratification at his convenience. Here are suggestions for dealing with the Fling Man.

Are You the Only One?

If you get together with a Fling Man less than once a week there's a good chance you're not the only women in his life. You have the right to ask him if he is seeing other women. If you're not in a monogamous relationship with a man, then you need to find out if he practices safe sex. If he is elusive and gives you some double-talk, then you have to consider if you want to be with a man who isn't willing to share this essential information. Not knowing if a man is having safe sex is self-destructive. Nowadays being in denial can be suicidal.

Janet, the women Fred met at the nightclub, asked if there were other women in his life. At first he was evasive and then he admitted that he was seeing two other women. He said that he was practicing safe sex, which she believed because he always used condoms with her.

Does He See a Future?

After a couple of months pass, you can ask him what he sees developing with the two of you. Rather than obsessing with your friends about why he calls you only occasionally, you can inquire about what his thoughts and fantasies are about the two of you in the future. You risk getting hurt but at least you'll know where you stand.

Janet asked Fred if he ever saw them having an exclusive relationship. Fred told Janet that he liked her very much, but he didn't know if he wanted to have an exclusive relationship with her or anyone in the near future.

Express Yourself

Make sure he knows exactly what you need, want, and expect from him. If you don't tell him, he'll never figure it out on his own. Here are a couple of examples:

Tell him he has to give you advance notice about getting together rather than calling just on a whim and when he feels like it.

Tell him you want to go out to places (restaurants, museums, films, dates) and not just get together for sex.

Janet told Fred that he would have to call her in advance when he wanted to get together rather than just asking her out on the spur of the moment. She also wanted to do more things together rather than just hang out in her apartment. Fred said that he liked being spontaneous but enjoyed Janet's company and wouldn't mind doing thing with her.

The Real World

Don't accept his reality as your reality! Just because he sees things a certain way doesn't mean you have to agree with him, or see it his way. Don't compromise on what you want. For example:

- Stick by your feelings and opinions about being in an exclusive relationship.

- Don't let him steamroll you with his possibly warped opinions on relationships and life.

Fred tried to explain to Janet why it's a good idea to date a lot of people at one time. He tried to reason with her that if they really dug each other they shouldn't be jealous if they saw other people. Janet stuck to her guns and said she disagreed with him, that it's normal to want an exclusive relationship. She felt it was healthy to want a man all to herself. In the end she did not surrender to his belief system.

The Limitations of Love

If you do set limits with the Fling Man, there is the possibility he will leave. With some Fling Men it's either his way or the highway. If this is the case, you'll have to decide if you want to relate to a man where everything's on his terms. Be aware that men who can't accept limits are usually impossible to have a healthy relationship with.Fred said that he didn't know if he could meet Janet's demands. He explained that he didn't like someone else telling him what to do or how to   live his life.

Progression

If a regular dating relationship doesn't develop in three months, it probably never will. After three months, if you're still waiting around for a normal dating relationship with the Fling Man, you're probably wasting your time and energy. Accept that your relationship is merely going to be a succession of flings.

When Fred couldn't tell Janet he would stop seeing the two other women and commit to her, at the three month mark, Janet decided to end her relationship with him. Fred still kept trying to convince her that things were okay the way they were. Janet stood by her guns and told him it was over. He tried to call a couple of times but he still had no intention of changing. She missed the good times they had together but she was committed to finding a man who wanted an exclusive relationship with a future. A year later she met George and within six months they got engaged.

How Do You Formulate Your Boundaries with the Fling Man?

Here are some questions for self-exploration to help you set stronger boundaries with the Fling Man.

You need to explore why you want to be with him. Are you re-enacting a historical relationship from your past?

- Why do you like jumping into a total merging situation?

- Why are you always so available?

- Why do you instantly meet his demands?

- Why are you so scared to set boundaries and say no?

- While you're waiting for the next phone call, are you trying to meet new men, live a productive life? Or are you wasting your life fantasizing about him?

You need to explore why charm means so much to you as a priority as opposed to other traits such as integrity, purpose in life, stability, and the future.

What Kind of Woman Is Able to Hook a Fling Man?

Not all women have the endurance or flexibility to deal with the Fling Man's meanderings, and you shouldn't feel like you have to. Here are some characteristics of those women who want to fight for him.

A woman who can endure the Fling Man's non-exclusivity.

- A woman who can endure the Fling Man's need to do his own things for however long that it takes, without knowing what he's doing.

- A woman who struggles with poor self-esteem, and doesn't feel entitled to be with a man who is accountable.

- A woman who has self-defeating needs and can endure emotional pain and suffering.

- A woman who's just not that crazy about him. (This meets the needs of two people who want a lot of distance automatically built in.)

- A woman who doesn't mind being involved with a man who may be involved with illegal activities.

- A woman who doesn't mind being with men who aren't steadily employed and is willing to financially support him occasionally (or all the time).

- A woman who doesn't mind that her needs are taken casually.

FIVE

THE ETERNAL BACHELOR

Martha was seeing Reade, a successful English professor. He was everything she was looking for in a potential mate. Sweet, fun to be with and a great conversationalist. He was also the same age as her, thirty-eight. They had been dating approximately six months when Reade told Martha that he had never lived with a woman and didn't want to ever get married. He explained that marriages usually didn't work and he didn't want to bother trying. Martha continued to see him anyway because despite what he said, he was a great boyfriend. She figured she'd worry about marriage later. Secretly, she hoped that the good times they were having together would change his ideas about the future. Another year passed and Reade told her he still had no intention of ever getting married.

Martha was crushed because she was almost forty now and wanted to have a child. She had no intention of becoming a single mom. When they discussed the issue, Reade said that having children just wasn't an important goal in his life. She was devastated that she had to break up with Reade now if she ever wanted to get married and have children. Despite the fact that she was in love with Reade, she now regrets that she had spent so much time with him. She thinks she should have listened when he told her he didn't want to marry from the beginning. She came to see me for a consultation because she was having a difficult time getting over him. I explained to Martha that she had been involved with an Eternal Bachelor.

Who Is the Eternal Bachelor?

The Eternal Bachelor is the emotionally healthiest of the categories described in this book because he has the capacity for a long-term relationship. However, he acts out his ambivalence by refusing to make a commitment to marriage despite his devotion to you.

Although he's basically a decent guy, the Eternal Bachelor is frustrating because a relationship with him will eventually lead to a tragic ending if marriage is your goal. The Eternal Bachelor is usually a pretty a good boyfriend, so it's easy to fall in love with him. He's not malicious or abusive. He just can't gratify your deep longing for permanence and family. He's particularly hard to walk away from because he may have given you a lot emotionally and physically. Unfortunately, holding on too long to the Eternal Bachelor with the hope that he's eventually going to come through for you will sometimes damage the health of the relationship, leading to a disastrous ending even though it was never his intent.

Signs of an Eternal Bachelor

If you are concerned about whether you are falling for an Eternal Bachelor, the following are the classic signs to be on the lookout for: r:

- **He's usually never been married.** It's a major sign if he's over forty years old. Some Eternal Bachelors have never even lived with a woman. Occasionally, they still live at home with their parents.

- **He is preoccupied with hobbies and self-interests.** Watch out for self-indulgent bachelor-type interests such as cars, clothes, extravagant vacations, endless working out at the gym, expensive electronic equipment, and so on. Try to imagine if he could sacrifice some of these pleasures to make time or emotional space for a marriage or family.

- **He never mentions children or having a family.** The Eternal Bachelor does not talk about wanting to have children and shows no apparent longings to be a dad. He's just not that interested in the entire subject of having a family.

- **He has a bachelor mind set.** He has a bachelor lifestyle, which he's comfortable with. His thinking is very "self"-oriented rather than "other"-oriented.

- **He doesn't mention the future with you.** When he talks about the future, it doesn't include you. On the rare occasion he mentions a possible fantasy wife she's usually vague, like a cartoon character. He has no apparent interest in building a life with another person.

- **He doesn't share information.** You'll never hear him talk about his money, properties, investments, background, etc., even though you've been together awhile. You have to really dig to get information out of him. Even when he's forthcoming, he'll often be defensive.

- **He's noncommittal.** He has a difficult time committing to events, going places, vacations, anything way in advance. If you bring up the subject, he gets quiet or at the very least doesn't enthusiastically join in.

- **You don't meet his family.** He doesn't invite you to meet his parents or family over holidays. If you hint about the subject, he'll come up with an excuse about why it's not a good idea.

- **You don't meet his friends.** He keeps his relationship with you separate from his social life with his friends. He mentions the other people in his life but he's not in any big rush for you to get together with them.

How the Eternal Bachelor Operates

The Eternal Bachelor has no problem attaching and forming a relationship—he just doesn't want to get married. When the subject of matrimony comes up with a woman he's involved with, he offers her the reasons he's rationalized to himself to justify his behavior and ward off his own feelings of guilt and/or anxiety. In other words, he defends his case for Eternal Bachelorhood. If one explanation isn't convincing enough, he'll move onto another one. The following are reasons the Eternal Bachelor doesn't want to marry, although he will not always disclose them to you when discussing the issue:

- **Fears the high divorce rate.** Often the Eternal Bachelor's biggest piece of evidence is that the divorce rate is very high, which is actually true. Approximately 60 percent of marriages end in divorce. He just doesn't want to take the chance of having to go through the emotional and financial devastation of a divorce.

- **Wants to be available to meet other women.** He doesn't want to totally close himself off from other women. He feels his dream woman may be right around the corner, and he wants the freedom to pursue the opportunity, should it arise. He wants to have one foot out the door at all times.

- **Doesn't want financial responsibility.** He doesn't want the financial burden of a wife and children. Even if you have a career, he'll still be responsible in the event you couldn't work for some reason. If things don't work out, he would have to pay child support and alimony, which makes him even more reluctant to take the risk.

- **Doesn't want to answer to anyone or make compromises.** It's true that if you marry and have a family, you *do* have to make compromises. He wants to be his own man and not be accountable to anyone.

- **Likes to do things himself.** He's very independent and likes to come and go as he pleases. Spending time by himself doing his own thing is important. Loneliness is not even an issue.

- **Likes his own space.** He doesn't like to share. He doesn't like anyone messing with his stuff and treasures his privacy.

- **Was hurt from past relationships.** He's been badly hurt from past relationships and would rather play it safe by not fully committing himself.

- **Wants to be only in romantic situations.** He loves the excitement of romance, seduction, and courtship but doesn't want the day-to-day routine of married life, which he's concerned could be boring. He's able to tolerate the continuity of a relationship up to a point.

- **Wants to learn more about himself or do his own thing.** He wants to devote his time and money to learning about himself, hobbies, traveling, and broadening his horizons. He doesn't want to put that all that energy into marriage or family.

- **Is married to his work.** Some Eternal Bachelors want to commit all their energy to their careers. They work a million hours a week and love every minute of it, not to mention all the money they're making.

- **Loves compromise.** Even though the Eternal Bachelor doesn't want to get married, deep down he still wants what every human being longs and craves for—intimacy. So he makes a compromise with his life. He gets himself into romantic situations where he gets his emotional and sexual intimacy needs met. However, he only gets involved in a relationship with a woman when he knows it won't work out. For this reason, it's common for him to get involved with women who are unavailable (they are married or involved with another man or woman, consumed with their career, addicted to drugs). Unfortunately, due to his ambivalence, he also gets involved with women who *are* totally available. Often, he doesn't let the available woman know he doesn't want to get married because she probably wouldn't go out with him if he volunteered this information up front.

- **Devalues you.** When he's deeply struggling with his ambivalence, he may devalue you to himself to rationalize his reasons not to marry. His tendency to devalue isn't as severe and distorted as the Runner, but like all of us, he may think about your faults and weigh them more heavily than a man who's serious about marriage as a goal in his life.

What Causes the Eternal Bachelor's Behavior?

Like many Ambivalent Men, the Eternal Bachelor has probably experienced something in his past that makes him fear intimacy.

The Eternal Bachelor may have had a mother who was enmeshed with him. Having felt smothered by his mother, he's afraid of being engulfed by a woman he loves. He needs to resolve his issues with his mother in order to emotionally separate from her and   fully commit himself to a woman.

If his parents were divorced when he was a child, he may have intense anxiety about going through the trauma again. He may be therefore reluctant to marry despite his longings for a relationship.

He may be afraid of becoming vulnerable and emotionally dependent, a situation that can develop from marriage. By staying single he won't have to grapple with these issues.

Sometimes, as Freud says, a cigar is just a cigar. Maybe he's having a great time being single. He's got money, a good job or great career, access to a lot of women. Nowadays, remaining single doesn't necessarily mean anything is wrong with him. He's just happy the way he is and doesn't want to give up his bachelor lifestyle no matter how strong his feelings are for you.

How to Handle the Eternal Bachelor

The Eternal Bachelor can be a handful to deal with, but if you're aggressive and prepared, you may be able to change his single ways.

Dispute His Rationalizations

My suggestion is to have only one major discussion with him where you dispute his rationalizations point for point. Be prepared. Don't be passive. Answer him back. (Examples: Life is a risk, some married people are happy, 40 percent of marriages *do* succeed, family life is good despite the odds.) Go for it, because you won't be arguing his rationalizations again.

Tell Him about It

Your dreams and goal of a wedding and family life are not unreasonable. Eternal Bachelors have the intellectual capacity to understand your needs and longing for marriage. They just have difficulty coming through for you in this area because of their own issues and beliefs. Be up front and put it out there. Don't be ashamed of who you are and what you want.

Fear Factor

The only reason an Eternal Bachelor would go beyond his comfort zone is the fear of losing you. However, if you put him in the position of having to make a choice, you also risk losing him. Some Eternal Bachelors would rather give up a woman they love than sacrifice the present lifestyle they enjoy or deal with their own intimacy issues and have to change.

Setting a "Time Limit"

So if you're dating an Eternal Bachelor almost a year already and there's no sound of wedding bells or talk of the future maybe you should consider giving him a "time limit"!

Tell him you want more than your present relationship. You want a future with someone. You don't want to keep schlepping around any more. Tell him you'll wait a certain amount of time. If at that point you're not engaged, you're walking.

Remember, it's a limit, not an ultimatum. You just don't want to invest any more time with a man who does not want to marry you and at that point you need to put your time and energy into looking for someone else who wants the same things in life as you do. It's what you have to do for you to get your long-term needs met.

Setting the limit will be difficult because you have to stick to your time limit, no matter how anxious and upset you become. If you don't adhere to your statements, you will lose your credibility with your Eternal Bachelor and stay stuck in the same go-nowhere situation without any change taking place.

Here are some pieces of advice that can help you avoid spending too much time with an Eternal Bachelor:

Listen to him.

When you're in the beginning stages of dating and he says he doesn't want to get married, take it seriously! When you give him the time limit and he still says he doesn't want to get married, listen to him then, too. Under either of these circumstances, if you do decide to see him anyway, you must know that you're gambling with time. It's your informed decision at this point, so don't make a victim out of yourself if things don't go your way.

Don't manipulate him!

If you're not happy with his decision, don't make a hysterical scene. Don't try to trick him by telling him you're pregnant. Deal with whom he really is and what he claims he wants.

Don't try to change him.

Argue with him about his rationalizations one time and that's it. Accept the fact that you both have different opinions about the subject. Listen to his beliefs even if you don't agree with them.

Be grateful.

If he tells you that he can't leave his bachelorhood behind, appreciate the fact that he's aware that marriage is not the best thing for him and he'd probably make a lousy husband anyway. You're better off ending it now before you get legally entangled or children are involved.

Greta, a thirty-three-year-old woman who wanted to get married, came to see me when she started dating Grady. She explained that dating had been a grueling experience for her. She was embarrassed to share that when she went on some of the blind dates she met through the personals, she felt that some of the men were disappointed when they met her.

She was finally introduced to Grady by a coworker. Grady turned out to be a devoted boyfriend. He took Greta on great dates and saw her every weekend. He had some faults that Greta was concerned about, but she felt that she loved him and could see herself spending the rest of her life with him. A year passed, however, and he never mentioned marriage or the future. Grady also had a lot of other Eternal Bachelor signs. He was self-focused, never mentioned a family, had a bachelor lifestyle, and withheld information about himself.

All Greta's sisters and relatives were married, and she wanted the same for herself. After a number of sessions and much contemplation, Greta decided to give Grady a time limit. That weekend she explained to him that she had invested a lot of time and energy in their relationship and she wanted to know where it was going. He said that he loved her but wasn't sure if he wanted to get married. She told him that she didn't want to keep dating for years and needed a commitment from him by the Christmas holidays. At that point, they had been dating for a year and a half. He listened but didn't have much of a reaction. Neither of them discussed the "time limit" for weeks even though Thanksgiving was just around the corner. On Christmas Eve, Grady presented Greta with a diamond engagement ring. They set a date and married the next June.

I have to tell you that giving a man a time limit doesn't always work out the way it did for Greta. I've known women to set a time limit and the guy bolts. The bottom line is: No suggestions are carved in stone. You have to do what you think is the best for you and your situation. Every man is different and will make his own individual decision. You have to feel right about the choices that you make, too. In the long run, you may be better off staying true to yourself and be willing to lose him for what you want.

Because if you stay with him and he doesn't eventually marry you (if marriage is what you want), it's likely you'll become resentful and angry, which may eventually destroy the relationship anyway.

SIX

The Ambivalent Cyber Man

Tanya was thrilled to be getting so many e-mails from men responding to her online personal ad. Her letter from Dave was different. It was warm, romantic, and sweet. He also sent a picture of himself with his son at Disneyland. Just turning forty-three, Tanya was unsure if she wanted to have a child so the thought of a stepson was very exciting to her. She was especially happy to see that Dave looked a little bit like John Travolta.

She answered his letter the next day and was surprised to hear from him again so quickly. He told her that he was divorced and that he had his own lawn maintenance business. Dave was sounding more like her dream man by the minute. She was thrilled when she went online the next night and he instant-messaged her. They began to chat and quickly hit it off. She laughed to herself, thinking how much this was like a date except they didn't hear each other's voices. They both agreed to a second cyberdate the next evening.

Tanya couldn't wait to get home from work and jump online. When eight o'clock arrived, her heart sank when she didn't see Dave's name flash up on her buddy list. About to sign off, she was relieved to see his instant-message box appear. Once again, they had a great chat. She thought by now he'd ask her for her phone number, but instead he just said he had to go. His last words were he'd be online the next night and signed off. She thought his not wanting to speak on the phone was strange but figured that's what people on the Internet did. The next night, as they chatted, she told Dave that she'd like to speak to him. Tanya was relieved when he asked for her number, promising to call the next evening. She never heard from Dave and, in fact, never saw him online ever again. Tanya had run into an Ambivalent Cyber Man!

Who Is the Ambivalent Cyber Man?

He's part of the Information Age gone wrong! This Ambivalent Man hides behind the computer screen to avoid relationships and intimacy. He can be anybody. The only way he can relate is in his house or apartment with words he's typing on a keyboard. He may even be afraid to speak with you on the phone. In the event he is who he says he is, and not a psycho making up another identity, he can be suffering from a plethora of problems. You'll never know because you'll never see him or speak with him.

Cindy met Mel in a chat room for writers. Mel's online profile indicated that they had a great deal in common. They both loved writing, the arts, films, books, and poetry. On paper he looked as though he could be her soul mate. Anxious to meet her possible dream man, Cindy started hinting around for them to get together. Whenever they made a plan to meet Mel would cancel, explaining that something came up. Finally, Cindy bluntly told him either they had to meet or they'd have to stop corresponding. They finally went out to dinner. Cindy was shocked when she saw that he looked nothing like his picture or the way he physically described himself. She figured the reason he was acting ambivalent about meeting her was that he was afraid to let her see that he was lying about himself.

How to Prevent Getting Swept Up with an Ambivalent Cyber Man

Ambivalent Cyber men have zero capacity to commit to a "real" relationship. Here are signs to be on the lookout for so you don't squander any of your precious time.

- **Make it real!** Do not e-mail or instant message (IM) with a man more than two times without getting his phone number. If he doesn't want to meet or talk on the phone by the second chat or e-mail, this a red flag there is something wrong. He is probably an Ambivalent Cyber Man. A man who is serious about wanting to meet a woman will want to exchange numbers quickly and meet as soon as possible.

- **Call the phone number to see if he really exists.** Instead of wasting days dreaming that a possible relationship is materializing, see if he really lives at the phone number or if he's an Ambivalent Cyber Man who's playing mind games.

- **If he doesn't call you, that's a bad sign.** If he doesn't call you after exchanging meaningful, romantic, seductive e-mails or IMs, he's clearly not serious about a relationship. He's more likely playing cyber mind games. Most men who are looking for a relationship will call you after corresponding with you online. If he starts the vanishing act from the start, it's a sign he's an Ambivalent Cyber Man

- **If you see him online a lot, look out!** If you're corresponding or even dating a man who's online a lot, be on the lookout. He may be talking to other women online the way he's talking with you. Sometimes these Ambivalent Cyber Men have multiple cyber girlfriends. They can be flirting with women all over the world—and there's nothing worse than a cyber womanizer.

- **Don't get seduced by a fantasy.** If you're going through a hard time yourself (a breakup, divorce, problems at your job), be careful. It's a vulnerable time for you so you might be more susceptible to being seduced into a fantasy by a man you don't really know, or have never seen or spoken to. So, even if you're feeling needy for love and attention, still try to get the cyber exchange offline to make it real rather than a fantasy.

- **Take him off your buddy list.** When you see his name on your buddy list you'll be compelled to instant message him, which will keep the whole cyber game going. If you don't see his name, at least you'll be more focused on trying to keep this a real connection that could lead to a real relationship, rather than keeping it at a cyber   fantasy level.

91

- **Don't have cyber sex!** No matter how lonely and vulnerable you feel, don't ever have cyber sex with a man you don't know. If it's your boyfriend, then it's none of my business; but if it's a man you've been e-mailing, or IM-ing online, be careful. Until you meet him, you don't really know who this is. For all you know it might not even be a man or an adult. Although it may seem exciting and a diversion from your problems, do not participate. Women who have had cyber sex with a man they knew only online have felt degraded and very regretful afterward.

He's Definitely a Cyber Ambivalent Man! What Do I Do?

An Ambivalent Cyber Man is a waste of time in the relationship department. Nothing will ever materialize with him. All he ever wants to do is flirt and play seductive head games. Sometimes he's primarily looking to engage in cyber sex. The bottom line is he's not serious about a real relationship. And worst of all, you don't know who or what you're dealing with. If you find yourself involved with an Ambivalent Cyber Man . . .

- **Stop communicating with him online.** Don't IM him or e-mail him. If you communicate with him, you're encouraging the ambivalent cyber cycle. So make sure you no longer put any energy into your cyber dating or hanging out with him online.

- **Do not respond if he IM's you.** If he tries to chat with you online, do not respond. You will just be encouraging this imaginary relationship that is going nowhere fast.

- **Try a new personal ad/online dating site.** If it's possible, try to take a break from the personal ad site where you met him. Seeing his picture up there may make it harder for you to forget him, so try to start over on another site, someplace where you won't be reminded of him.

Later in the book, I do suggest that women use the personal ad sites online to meet men. I've known many women who have met the men they date and marry through these sites. But always be wary of Ambivalent Men who utilize these sites to meet women and play heads games, flirt, and act out their hostility and ambivalence, rather than peruse a serious, healthy, long-term relationship with a woman.

Lyn was having a hard time getting out because she's a single mom with two children of preschool age. She was thrilled when her mother bought her a new computer for her birthday. Enthusiastic to meet men online, she quickly learned how to work the Internet. She put her ad on three personal-ad sites. She got lots of responses but was especially interested in Artie, a handsome widowed fireman with two kids of his own. She e-mailed him and was thrilled to hear from him within an hour. They kept e-mailing each other and then finally spoke on the phone. Although he lived only twenty miles away, he never seemed to be able to meet for a date. Having been in my support group, Lyn figured she was dealing with an Ambivalent Man. Frustrated, she went back to the drawing board and answered some more responses to her online personal ad. A lot of the guys played cyber games with her, just IM-ing and e-mailing but never getting it together for a real date. Then she read Charlie's letter. He was funny and romantic. She quickly wrote back to him. After they e-mailed once he asked if he could call her. They spoke that very night and he asked her to go out to dinner Saturday evening. They totally hit it off and within a month they were living together. Whenever anybody complains to Lyn about not meeting men, she always suggests that they should try to meet men in cyber space.

SEVEN

Why Do You Keep Falling for Ambivalent Men?

You're a smart woman. You can see the truth clearly for your friends or other women, but when it comes to your own choices, sometimes it's hard to see the forest through the trees. The right answer could be staring you right in the face, and you don't even know it! When it comes to career, children, and life in general, you've got it wired. So why are you so off the mark with your choices in men? The following reasons will help you understand why you keep falling for an Ambivalent Man.

You're Terrified of Being Alone

The fear of being alone will cause you to stay with a man no matter how hopeless the relationship. Does this sound like you? You'd rather be with a man who hurt or betrayed you than face being alone. Spending time with yourself and waiting to meet a man who is capable of a healthy relationship is not even an option. Whoever is there for the moment to fill up the empty void will do.

Your terror and pain is sometimes so profound that the humiliation or psychological pain of being with a man who gives only a part of himself and won't commit to you is preferable to being by yourself. The only way to break out of this vicious cycle is to build your sense of self so you can tolerate being alone.

Your Initial Selection Process Might Be Flawed

You need to take a good look at how you initially select men to date. What a woman finds appealing in a man when she first meets a him may distort her ability to see whether a man has the capacity for an enduring, stable relationship. Here are two behaviors that strongly contribute to a woman's falling for an Ambivalent Man:

1. **Focusing more on a man's physical appearance and superficial qualities than on his character.** You know that he's not good relationship material, but you get enthralled with his disarming charm and seductive powers and forget to check out his character. You may be missing out on a quality man who would make a great boyfriend or husband because you're so

busy thinking about a man's appearance rather than his maturity level or if he's a keeper.

Women talk about how men can objectify women, but women can also objectify men by just having mental blueprints of how men must look before they even consider dating them. Women limit themselves from finding potential mates by focusing only on their packaging. This approach can lower your chances of meeting a man who is capable of enduring and healthy love. For example, Celia openly admits that she will only date men who have a full head of hair and are over 5'10" (she's 5'3"). She meets and dates a lot, but if a man does not meet her criteria, she immediately crosses him off the list as a potential mate. However, she is often depressed that she's alone and can't become part of a couple.

2. **Splitting men into two categories: sexy and exciting versus nerdy and boring.** You have a hard time seeing that some men can have a mixture of qualities and are not necessarily one or the other. You immediately get rid of men who may have the potential to have a solid healthy relationship because they are not exciting or cool enough. You put men into categories rather than seeing them as whole human beings. You're much more focused on a man's ability to stimulate you rather than whether or not he's supportive

and capable of a long-term relationship. Boredom for you is a fate worse than death.

Beverly wanted to get married in the worst way, but she would let herself get involved only with men she thought were sexy, and she would always end up disappointed. She felt that most of the men she met who wanted a long-term relationship were too boring and nerdy. They weren't as fashionable or hip as the sexy guys. She'd often cry herself to sleep because she wanted to be in a relationship so badly. Still, she vowed she wouldn't spend even a moment with a nerd, and she often soothed herself with chocolate ice cream.

These two behaviors and ways of thinking will make you more vulnerable to falling for Ambivalent Men. In later chapters, I will discuss how to work on changing these behaviors if you wish to do so.

Your Priorities Are Different from Other Women's

Women who fall for Ambivalent Men often have priorities different from those women who do not fall for Ambivalent Men. Many women who fall for Ambivalent Men are more focused on short-term gratification. They have a difficult time tolerating the frustration, patience, and loneliness they must endure while waiting to meet a man who is available and capable of a long-term relationship. They get whatever emotional, physical, or material gratification they can out of relationships, even when they know there's no future or hope for marriage and family. When a woman decides to get together with an Ambivalent Man she may rationalize to herself that "it's just a fling" or "I work hard all day so I deserve to have this fun even if there's no future." She doesn't mind risking the time she's spending with him even though the odds of a building a long-term relationship look terrible.

For instance, Eileen was willing to get involved in a clandestine affair with a married man who took her on vacations to exotic islands, even though she knew there was no future with him. She rationalized that she was having a great time seeing new places and acquiring new possessions she couldn't afford on her own. Meanwhile, she was miserable when she spent holidays and birthdays alone while he was off with his wife and children. She compromised her hopes and dreams for marriage, settling for crumbs rather than the whole loaf.

Women who don't fall for Ambivalent Men are much more focused on the long-term goal of marriage. In addition to wanting a husband to love and be loved by, their strong desire for marriage is sometimes due to a variety of other reasons including these:

- Wanting to conform to society and be part of a couple (being single is still a minority and not the norm)
- Wanting to have a spouse or partner to take to business functions or social engagements
- Wanting to please their family
- Wanting to boost their career (when being married might improve their image)
- Not wanting to be alone
- Wanting people to know you're "loved" or "chosen"

Making marriage a major priority will make the immediate gratification of being with someone with great chemistry but who can't commit, fall to the wayside. Changing your priorities can also change who you want to get involved with.

Stella was dating Joe, a man who had just been released from jail for committing a white-collar crime. He was handsome and charismatic but never finished college and didn't have any prospects for a big career. Stella, on other hand, graduated from

Harvard and was earning a six-figure salary working as a loan officer. They really didn't have much in common, but Joe was a blast and Stella loved dancing and partying with him. When she went home for Thanksgiving, she was jealous of her friends who were able to bring husbands and children home to their family gatherings and wondered why she was still spending so much of her time with a man she knew she had no intention of ever marrying. When she realized that getting married was an essential goal for her, her priorities shifted and so did the men she dated.

You Don't Feel a Sense of Entitlement

You can follow all the dating rules in the world from all the relationship experts till you're blue in the face, but if you don't feel that you're entitled to thoughtful, loving, consistent behavior, you'll end up vulnerable to Ambivalent Men. Even if you try to behave in a prescribed way, unless you have that sense of entitlement, your anxiety and self-doubt will start to kick in and you'll find yourself putting up with the Ambivalent Man's shenanigans.

If you've ever listened to Ellen Fein and Sherrie Schneider, who wrote *The Rules: Time-Tested Secrets for Capturing the Heart of Mr. Right* (Warner Books, 1995), being interviewed on TV, it's obvious they have a strong sense of entitlement. It appears they feel worthy and deserving of a man who wants to be with them and treats them with respect and consideration, so it's easy for them to preach their "Rules."

Do you feel entitled to a man who wants to see you on the weekends? Wants to marry you after you've dated for around a year? Who is consistent and doesn't abandon you? Women who are in happy, satisfying relationships and marriages often tend to feel that they are entitled to the love and relationship they are receiving—that they wouldn't settle for anything less.

How Your Parents Influenced You

Our radar seeks out men who remind us of our parents. If you come from a dysfunctional family, you're likely to be attracted to dysfunctional partners. It could be difficult for you to recognize a man who has problems or is abusive when you meet him. You may seek (consciously or unconsciously) men who would treat you the same way your parents did because you are looking for the familiar. The unknown (stable, consistent, healthy, reciprocated love) is foreign to you.

Mothers

A woman's relationship with her mother has a strong effect on her choices of men and the way she relates to them. You might have a tendency to fall for Ambivalent Men as a result of the following circumstances:

- **Your mother was ambivalent.** She became emotionally involved with you and would suddenly distance, seeming disinterested or even provoking an argument.

- **Your mother falls for Ambivalent Men.** Your mother is your role model, so if she has a history of getting involved with Ambivalent Men (this can include your father), then you have learned this behavior from her.

- **Your mother is competitive with you** (yes, believe it or not, mothers can be competitive with their daughters). You're afraid that if you have a successful relationship you will outshine her, resulting in her getting angry and rejecting or abandoning you.

- **Your mother has had horrible relationships with men that were filled with deprivation and**

103

pain. You're afraid that if you have a successful relationship, you will feel guilty that you have more than she has. As a result, you choose Ambivalent Men to be assured your lack of success.

- **Your mother was emotionally or physically abusive to you.** You're used to relationships filled with pain and chaos. You're able tolerate abusive behavior from men because of its familiarity.

Angelina's mother had behaved completely ambivalent toward her since she was a little girl. Because Tanya's father took off right after she was born, her mother raised her all by herself. Her mother took an occasional serious interest in Angelina's life. One year, her mother went to parent-teacher's night. Sometimes she even checked Angelina's homework. Then, all of a sudden she'd flip-flop and be completely disinterested in Angelina, showing no concern for what was going on in Angelina's life. Her mother dated a lot, and it was when her mother didn't have a boyfriend that she paid more attention to Angelina. However, the moment she was involved with a man she'd do a 180-degree turn and barely take care of Tanya. As Angelina got older, she and her mother were often very competitive. Her mother often made critical remarks about

Angelina's clothes and figure. When Angelina started to date, her mother always picked on her boyfriends, making Angelina feel humiliated and criticized.

Angelina didn't really think much about her mother's confusing behavior until she realized that she too kept getting involved with men who always left her. They seemed as though they were into her and then they'd lose interest, only to change their minds and be interested in her again. Angelina started wondering why she kept attracting these mixed-up guys. It was when she joined the women's group I run that she started remembering her mother's ambivalent behavior toward her. She realized that the men she was dating were replicas of her mother.

Keep in mind that you have to give up the old dysfunctional relationship you may have had with your mother while growing up, if you want to be with an available man who is able to have a fully committed, loving relationship with you. If you let go of the dysfunctional relationship with a man, in a way it's letting go of your mother and truly emotionally separating from her. Even though Angelina felt her mother was not a good nurturing mother, she was still deeply attached to her. When she was growing up she didn't have any brothers or sisters, so all they had was each other. So, for Angelina to let go of Ambivalent Men was to truly emotionally separate from her mother. This is hard work, however, and often easier said than done. For Angelina it was well worth the effort because after she worked through some of the issues about her mother, she became involved with Ian, who was much more attentive and emotionally available.

Fathers

Freud, the father of psychology, said in his book *Civilization and Its Discontents:* "I cannot think of any need in childhood as strong as the need for a father's protection." If you have been rejected or abandoned by your father either emotionally or physically, then it is most likely that you will have issues with the men you choose to become involved with and the relationships you create with them.

In addition, if you have experienced any of the following circumstances with your father, you may have a tendency to fall for Ambivalent Men:

- **Your father was ambivalent toward you.** He might have occasionally been warm and close to you and would then pull away.

- **Your father was ambivalent toward your mother, which you observed and learned.** Now you think that's how all men relate to women.

- **Your father wasn't emotionally available** because he was preoccupied with his work, leaving you feeling rejected and abandoned.

- **Your father physically abandoned you and your family.** You might choose men who are unreliable and will ultimately abandon you because you believe that if your father didn't want to stick around when you were a child, then no man will want to.

- **Your father was often rejecting toward you when you were a child or adolescent.** He didn't take much interest in you or spend enough time with you. You're likely to choose Ambivalent Men who are occasionally rejecting or limited in how much time they spend with you.

- **Your father was physically and/or emotionally abusive to you.** You're now vulnerable to men who are abusive because you're accustomed to this behavior. Women who don't have abusive fathers usually run away from abusive men.

- **If your father was flirtatious or in any way seductive to you** (without actually sexually acting out) you may be drawn to men who always relate with sexual undertones. You might find men who are down to earth and not flirtatious not stimulating enough for you.

- **If your father was sexually abusive to you, you'll have a tendency to choose men who are completely dysfunctional and are incapable of loving in a mature healthy way.** If you have been sexually abused, the best way to recover is through psychotherapy.

Do any of these descriptions of fathers sound like your father? Choosing men who do not have the ways of your dear old dad is a way to emotionally separate from him. It's hard to let go of your original love (your father) and familiar ways of relating, no matter how dysfunctional they are.

Lindsay had a great relationship with her dad until she turned eleven, when her parents divorced. Her father was working overtime to pay for his own apartment, alimony, and child support. Between all the hours he was putting in at the office and living in his own place, Lindsay hardly had a chance to see him. When he did take her out on Sundays, they often got into an argument, something they never did before. Then he started dating a woman whom he quickly married. His new wife, Sheila, quickly got pregnant and before Lindsay knew it, she had a stepsister. Lindsay's father had less and less time for her and they grew father apart. Lindsay remembers feeling rejected by her father's lack of interest but was too embarrassed to say anything. She figured if he loved her, she shouldn't have to remind him to spend time with her.

When Lindsay got older and started to date, she only chose men who never had enough time to see her. They either had another girlfriend or were very committed to their careers. When she went to see a therapist, she was told that she kept repeating the relationship she had with her father by getting involved with men who were essentially unavailable.

The urge to repeat trauma is often more powerful than the search for a healthy, reciprocated love. The famous British psychoanalyst W. R. D. Fairbairn found that when children were abused by their parents and taken to a foundling home, they would rather go back to their abusive parents than stay in the safety of the foundling home. So, if you're familiar with bad treatment from your family members (or good treatment), you will be naturally drawn to the same behavior. It's what you're used to and comfortable with. The more you read psychological literature, the more you learn how alluring familiarity is—no matter how painful it is.

Freud also spoke about repetition compulsion. He explained that we all have a need to repeat the past and try to repair what was problematic from our childhoods. Unfortunately, we can't fix the adult replicas of our parents (the men we choose). The best we can do is try to find healthier men to help us heal some of the damage that has already been done.

How Other Family Members Influenced You

Though your parents were an important influence on your preference for men who can't commit, other members of your family also had an impact. Your siblings and other mother figures (aunts and grandmothers) can play a large role in your relationships as an adult.

Brothers

Your brother's behavior while you were growing up has a tremendous impact on your choice of men in your adult life. If you were humiliated or degraded by your brother by teasing or by emotional, physical, or sexual abuse, you might be vulnerable to continuing to accept this kind of behavior from men you have relationships with. In other words, if you've been victimized as a sister, you might continue to be victimized by men. So, if you keep falling for Ambivalent Men but have loving supportive parents, then maybe you should take a look at how your brother treated you. Women also report that having great relationships with their brothers in childhood has helped them to get involved with healthier men in their adult lives. A strong male sibling presence can help women to realize that there are men out there who are capable of healthy love and relationships.

Lola has a brother who was always supportive of her. Even though their parents had severe drinking problems, she and her brother always knew that they had each other. Even now, when Lola feels frustrated about her "man problems," she knows she'll always feel better just giving her "ol' bro" a call and hearing his voice. Their talks always cheers her up and give the strength to keep dating because she knows there are some "good guys" out there, especially since her brother is one of them.

Sisters

Women who have had sisters that were in any way abusive can be left traumatized and scarred. As a result, they might get involved with dysfunctional men because they were used to being close to a sibling who was awful to them.

The behaviors your sister had that could be affecting you today may include these:

- Being physically abusive to you (pulling your hair, hitting, slapping, or punching you)
- Picking on you, especially if you are younger than her
- Constantly ignoring you
- Sexually abusing you
- Constantly rejecting you
- Always demanding attention from your parents

Every time Joan even thinks about her sister Hannah, she starts to get stomach cramps. When she first came to my office, Joan told me that her sister had suffered from emotional problems as far back as she could remember. While they were growing up, Hannah would sometimes start cursing and insulting Joan. Sometimes her sister would even grab Joan's hair. Joan hoped it would never happen again, but Hannah would suddenly get crazy and physically attack her. Eventually Hannah was diagnosed with borderline personality disorder.

Although Joan completely understands how much her sister was suffering, she can't help but wonder if some of her own poor choices in men could be a result of growing up with Hannah and never feeling completely safe. Her last two boyfriends' behaviors were sometimes just as erratic as her sister's. She never really felt safe with either of them, always wondering when the next shoe was going to drop.

Aunts

Aunts can be like second mothers. I spend a lot of time with my eleven-year-old niece and am always telling her how wonderful, talented, and pretty she is. I know that the love I give her and my positive messages are already helping her develop confidence and strengthen her sense of self. I want her to have a sense of entitlement by the time she starts dating boys.

I've also heard from other women how their aunts were there for them in ways that their mothers weren't, making a positive impact on their self-esteem, and ultimately affecting their choices in men and how they relate to them. Think about the female family members in your past. Did you have aunts who were there for you? Even if they didn't do anything earth-shattering, just their presence alone could have had some impact if they were nice to you—gentle, nurturing, wise, and motherly. If they treated you as if you weren't important or criticized you in any way, that could also have had an effect on your self-esteem. How they related to men could have also served as a model for you. Do you have any memories of how your aunts got along with your uncles or your father (if he's her brother)?

Grandmothers

There's nothing like a wonderful grandma to clean up the mess your mother made by her ambivalent or dysfunctional behavior. Grandmas can be like second mothers. By taking a look at your grandmother and her relationships, you may be able to learn more about your mother's relationships, and possibly even your own. Sometimes grandmas can be even better mothers because they have the experience of raising children and the emotional distance of not being your mother. So, as you did with your aunts, think about your grandma's behavior. Do you have any memories of her being kind, mean, nurturing, critical, loving, or abusive? Do any of these behaviors have an effect on your sense of self and your self-image as a woman today?

What kind of role model was your grandmother in terms of how she related to men? Did she have a good stable marriage or was she with men who were ambivalent? Were the men unfaithful and incapable of staying married or committed to her, or were they and reliable? Did you see your mother repeating these types of relationships? Are you repeating these types of relationships? Sometimes women's issues with men can be generational.

How Your Adolescence Influenced You

Think back to your teenage years. Did anything traumatizing happen to you then? Did you date? What was your experience like being with boys? The answers to these questions can give you clues to why you for fall for Ambivalent Men. Your experiences as an adolescent might also be affecting your relationships with men in your adult life. If you experienced traumas during your teenage years, they still could be playing a part in the choices you make in men and relationships. Take a look at the following issues to see if any of them are still affecting you today.

Switching High Schools

Switching high schools can be an especially traumatic experience for any teen. If you had to switch high schools as a result of a divorce or a move, you may have found it difficult to start fresh and make new friends. As a result, you probably felt isolated and rejected by classmates who knew each other and were already in cliques. This could have led to you to feel socially inadequate as a teenager, making you feel less confident with men as an adult woman today.

'

You Were Tormented by Other Girls in High School

Many studies have documented what a powerful effect being tormented by other girls can have on teenage girls. You can carry this trauma with you into adulthood. Childhood teasing and bullying is damaging to a girl's self-image. You may have felt traumatized and been affected in the following ways:

- You suffered lowered self-esteem.
- You had less confidence in yourself when relating to boys.
- You didn't have enough emotional energy left to even think about dating boys.
- You might have even been afraid to date boys from your school for fear of retribution from the other   girls.

The trauma that results from these scenarios could have effected your adolescent development in regard to dating and boys. You might still be walking around as an adult with the same self-image you had then.

You Had a Severe Weight Problem

Many women I've worked with report that they had a severe weight problem, which affected their social lives in high school. Some of these women still carry that image of themselves today, even though they are not currently struggling with their weight. Trisha was a size twenty-two all through high school. Because she hardly dated, she ate more and more, trying to forget her loneliness and feelings of rejection. It was a vicious cycle. When she graduated from college, she went to Weight Watchers and lost over 100 pounds. Now she's a size six. No matter how much attention she gets from men now, however, she can't let go of her image of being an overweight teenager who teenage boys weren't that interested in. When she meets a man who's attracted to her, she feels so grateful for his attention that she

117

desperately clings to him no matter how he treats her. Trisha had to go for counseling to learn how to let go of her old memory of herself as a lonely sixteen-year-old and begin seeing herself as a glamorous twenty-eight-year old woman, which is how she realistically appears to everyone else. The way she related to men became healthier as soon as her self-image shifted.

You Suffered a Tremendous Loss

Living through the chaos of divorce or the death of an immediate family member can cause a teenager to feel abandoned and betrayed. If you suffered the trauma of a tremendous loss, it could have affected your teenage years and relationships with boys. As an adult the trauma you experienced as a teenager could still be affecting your choices in men and the way you relate to them.

For instance, Rita's mother died when she was five. Although Rita and her father got along great, she always felt as if there was something missing in her life. When she dated in her twenties, she was always afraid her boyfriends were going to just disappear. Due to this fear she often acted very clingy, presenting herself as a woman with little confidence in herself. After much soul-searching she realized it was the earlier loss of her mother that was triggering her desperate behavior.

How Stressful Life Circumstances Affect You Today

All of the following situations can make a woman feel so desperate for emotional relief and connection that it becomes almost impossible for her to wait for a man who is emotionally together, healthy, and reliable. Examine them closely. Do any of these circumstances fit with your relationship patterns?

Money Issues

Any type of situation in which you don't have the resources to fully support yourself financially can make you much less demanding and more willing to put up with bad behavior. Perhaps you've recently lost your job. Maybe you're having the trouble paying the bills. Perhaps you've been abandoned by your husband, you don't have child support or alimony, and you lack the training or skills to better yourself.

When you're having very severe money issues the stress of your situation may cause you to feel needy and tolerate ambivalent behavior from a man. You're so busy thinking about survival, a man's intimacy issues and erratic behavior can seem irrelevant. Therefore, you're much less demanding and more willing to put up with bad behavior from him.

Needing to Be There for the Children

If you're a single mom trying to take care of your kids, the need to be with your children and know that they are safe takes priority over relationships. In this case, you might prefer a man who is willing to just come over to the house and spend time with you so you don't have to worry about getting a babysitter and leaving your children alone in the evening. Because single moms are under so much stress worrying about their kids, managing their lives, dealing with their ex-husbands, paying the bills, and holding down the fort, an Ambivalent Man's behavior takes less precedence in their lives. A single mom may not have a lot of opportunities to get out, so if an Ambivalent Man drops in once in awhile, it's more convenient for her. Because she enjoys the little break from her life the Ambivalent Man offers, whatever attention she gets, however little, seems better than nothing. Therefore, she is more willing to put up with unsupportive or inconsistent behavior, or she may rationalize that it doesn't matter if there's not a future.

Health Problems

If you are suffering from a chronic health problem, you deserve a man who is very understanding of your limitations. Women who are suffering with chronic pain problems or chronic illness may suffer from low self-esteem, believing that their chances of getting or keeping a man are lessened by their physical limitations. Some women who suffer from health problems may be more apt to put up with any kind of behavior a man dishes out because it's harder to meet men given her condition. She feels grateful that he's even seeing her, despite his negative qualities or his faults.

Jo Ann's back problems became so severe she had to go on disability. She met Nick at a bar when her friends insisted they take her out to a local pub for her birthday. Nick was sitting on the chair right next to hers. They started talking and hit it off immediately. When she let him know that she was out of work and very limited in her physical activity, she was relieved that it didn't bother him at all. They started to date, but after a few months he started acting very ambivalent—not calling consistently, forgetting dates. Normally she wouldn't tolerate that kind of behavior, but she was so glad to have his companionship she over looked his hurtful behavior. She decided she would just put up with his antics until she felt better. She told herself that she was in no condition to go looking for another man while she was in all this pain.

Even if you are struggling with chronic pain or illness, you don't have to tolerate a man who isn't respectful of you and your needs. There are men out there who are struggling with their own limitations, who have the emotional maturity and capability to be completely understanding of a woman's limitations. You're better off being alone and getting your companionship needs met in a variety of other ways (children, friends, coworkers) than being with a man who treats you poorly.

Catastrophic Problems

Recent world events make the possibilities of catastrophic problems more of a reality. The loss of an apartment or house, a terrorist attack, or the loss of loved ones can cause feelings of loneliness and despair that may drive you to seek comfort in the arms of an Ambivalent Man, perhaps one who you cast away long ago.

Although this sounds dramatic, in the aftermath of 9/11, many of my clients who lived in New York City called men from their pasts they swore they'd never talk to again (they weren't in touch with them for years). The fact that they were contacting Ambivalent Men was temporarily irrelevant. At the time, they felt the need for connection so badly that getting in touch with someone familiar was all that counted. Everything else paled in comparison. Some women felt so traumatized that they couldn't see they were going to regret in a few months contacting Ambivalent Men from their past.

In times of trouble and tragedy, it's natural to seek out comfort. However, it's healthier to seek comfort from friends, family, and those who love you. If you have the urge to call an Ambivalent Man from your past, you must be willing to accept the severe emotional consequences that may occur down the line. Give yourself a few days before making the call and think about your situation. Chances are, after several days have passed, you'll realize that you have the emotional strength to resist opening up a potentially messy can of worms.

Empower Yourself Now

Do any of the issues I've just outlined fit your situation with an Ambivalent Man? If you can't relate and continue to totally blame Ambivalent Men, you're fooling yourself. You are not a victim! Yes, you may feel more vulnerable than the next woman due to some of these issues, but they don't make you any less worthy of having a trusting, loving relationship with a man.

By putting all of the responsibility on the Ambivalent Man, you are empowering him. Remember that the Ambivalent Man is not your higher power. He's just a man with issues, some even deeply pathological.

So, rather than feeling victimized, use this book to gather insights so that you can empower yourself. If you're with an Ambivalent Man, be there out of choice rather than need or desperation. Here are some ways for you to start working on empowering yourself now:

Keep working on getting out of the stressful life circumstances that make you vulnerable to Ambivalent Men.

- Keep working on increasing your self-awareness so that you become less vulnerable to Ambivalent Men.
- Stop feeling like a victim! Take responsibilities for your willingness to accept the Ambivalent Men's behavior.
- Keep reading this book.
- Observe women (both single and married) who aren't vulnerable to the behavior of Ambivalent Men. See how they cope, and make an effort to incorporate these actions into your own life.

- Try to imagine life without the stress of an Ambivalent Man's confusing behavior while you're struggling with your present life issues.

- Try not to reach out to your Ambivalent Man the next time you feel insecure or during your next crisis. Instead, see how you get through it on your own. Get to know how it feels to have emotional space free of your Ambivalent Man. Try not to contact him! This will be a great emotional exercise!

- Internalize new role models rather than the one's you've had since childhood. Read books and articles and see movies about women who make it through all sorts of life circumstances without depending on a man.

- Read any books that will positively strengthen and enlighten you—self-help books, memoirs, spiritual books.

- Write ten positive affirmations about yourself and repeat them every day.

- Visualize yourself in a happy healthy relationship with a man who's not acting ambivalent, who's sure of his love for you, and who doesn't disappoint   or betray you. See it, feel it, taste it!

- Visualize yourself being successful getting through stressful circumstances on your own. Imagine yourself as a powerful, independent woman (which you are although you may not know it yet). See it, feel it, taste it.

EIGHT

WHY DO YOU STAY WITH AMBIVALENT MEN?

Although some women fall for Ambivalent Men, not all women stick around to endure their wishy-washy, provocative, ambivalent behavior. But why do some women stay with them no matter how bad things get? Through conducting numerous workshops and private sessions with patients, I've come to discover that women who get entrenched in relationships with Ambivalent Men have a particular pattern of behaviors and ways of thinking. Read through this chapter to see if you can identify with any of the ten behavior traits or thinking processes I describe. If you identify with any of them, you could be in danger of sticking by an Ambivalent Man!

Magical Thinking

Magical thinking means hanging in there, hoping and expecting a man to miraculously change no matter how many times he disappoints you. It is the most prevalent of all the behaviors patterns of women who have a severe problem walking away from an Ambivalent Men.

If you engage in magical thinking, you're unrealistically optimistic and delude yourself about his ambivalent behavior, because you don't want to face the reality that he's completely hopeless. Admitting that a relationship is not working means you'll have to end the relationship. However, if a you keep telling yourself that a man's going to change, you put off the pain of knowing that it's not going to work out. Magical thinking is a way of avoiding the dreaded loss and rejection of losing your Ambivalent Man.

For example, you've been dating a man who tells you he's not ready to get married and still lives with his mother. A year passes and he still doesn't show you any concrete evidence that he's ready for marriage. You hope against hope he'll magically change. Before you know it another two years have passed, you're still with him, he's still with his mother, and you're still not married. Or you don't hear from him for days at a time and you never see him on the weekends. Rather than realizing that he can't make a commitment or that he's seeing other women, you choose to ignore his unavailable behavior, telling yourself he's going to change and eventually commit to you.

This type of behavior can lead to feelings of regret over wasting years of your life on a man you hoped against hope would change his ways. You deny and rationalize in order to keep convincing yourself that your man is going to do a complete turnaround. It doesn't usually happen that way. What you see is what you get. The only way a man will change is if he commits himself to serious psychotherapy and goes consistently. Even then it's hard to change. Just look at how hard it is for *you* to change.

High Tolerance for Emotional Pain

Do you tolerate whatever bad treatment a man dishes out as long as you have some part of him, even if it's just the crumbs? Do you put up with his stalling for time to get engaged or married and tolerate the frustration and his rejection without putting your foot down and telling him to get lost? If so, you are probably subjecting yourself to unnecessary emotional pain.

For instance, some women passively tolerate a man abandoning her or even seeing other women while he's seeing her rather than stand up for herself and set limits. If you put up with this type of behavior, you may be struggling with self-esteem issues. A woman who has a strong sense of herself would find this pain too unbearable and instead would walk out or confront him, regardless of possibly losing him or the relationship.

You Blame Yourself, Not the Man, for Rejection

Do you find yourself turning your anger inward rather than see his criticism or rejection of you as his rationalization for his own inability to have a meaningful long-term relationship? He thinks it's your fault that the relationship can't last (due to whatever he criticizes about you) rather than taking responsibility for his own anxiety about relationships and commitment. And you buy into it!

You know he's done things to provoke you to leave him (he cheats on you or has a tantrum and walks out on you). Instead of looking at these behaviors as his issues (his inability to have on ongoing healthy functional relationship), you start obsessing over how you might have provoked him. You think about how if you had been more careful, more gentle, more sensitive to his feelings, then maybe he wouldn't have left you. If only you had pleased him more! If you keep blaming yourself, you keep staying with men who are incapable of healthy long-term relationships because you can't see them for who they truly are and their own commitment problems.

You Have a Hard Time Seeing or Accepting His Emotional Limitations

You're more focused on your fantasy of who you would like him to be rather than the reality of who he really is. For instance, even though he's told you he's an alcoholic, you are shocked when he goes on a drinking binge. Or he tells you he's suffering from manic depression but you sweep his illness under the rug because he acts normal most of the time. Yet you are hysterical and bewildered when he gets into a manic phase and charges your credit cards to the limit.

No matter how intense your feelings are for him, it's essential that you're realistic about him. What you see is what you get. Trying to make believe his problems and his limitations don't exist will only catch up with you later on. Going into a relationship with your eyes wide open helps sharpen your judgment.

You Forgive Him Too Easily and Excuse His Negative, Hurtful Behavior

It's hard to resist when he begs you for forgiveness after he's broken your heart over and over. You feel loved and validated by his apology for the terrible mistake he's made after he's hurt you or rejected you repeatedly. It's important to remember that a man who has a pattern of repeatedly leaving (or provoking you to leave him) and remorsefully coming back, asking for your forgiveness, is probably compulsively acting out a deep-rooted psychological problem that would require years of psychotherapy to resolve. The bottom line is you must stop gratifying this back-and-forth behavior because breaking up and making up with the same person over and over is emotionally draining and very time-consuming. Let him go so you can move on to a man who is more emotionally stable and less damaged.

You're Gullible

He's lied to you again and again and yet you believe anything he tells you. You hope against hope that he's telling you the truth this time and you take everything he says to you at face value, even if you know intuitively that he might be making a fool out of you. You're afraid of confronting him about the truth because you're afraid he will leave you if you don't collude with his lies. You're also afraid that knowing the truth will make it to unbearable for you to stay with him. You let him smooth things over with you so you can both pretend everything is okay.

For instance, Sandy was dating a man who told her he was living with his grandmother. She never saw him on the weekends and he never answered the phone. Even though she was suspicious that his phone was only voice mail and that he was probably living with a woman who was not his grandmother, she didn't want to face the truth, preferring to believe his story. Eventually she found out that he was indeed married and felt foolish and angry with herself for not trusting her intuition.

You Tolerate Chaos and Unpredictability Even When It Inconveniences You

You have a great bonding experience with him and then he vanishes. He provokes an argument, storms out, and doesn't return for another month despite your frantic phone calls. He's always in a crisis (drugs, financial problems, legal problems). You can't depend on him. You somehow manage to tolerate his inconsistent behavior and chaotic life despite the draining effect his emotional disorganization has on your life. Using rationalization and denial, you manage to endure the pain of detaching from him over and over again.

For instance, Josephine started dating Billy, a guy with a super personality. She never knew when she was going to hear from him, though. They'd go out and then he'd stay over and call her nonstop for two days. Then he seemed to disappear off the face of the earth. Afterward he'd start calling again and almost move into her apartment, only to vanish again. Last week he told Josephine he was coming over to see her. She cleaned her apartment, excited about the visit because she hadn't seen him in awhile. Billy never showed up. Josephine was able to quickly forgive him when he apologized. She confronted him on his unpredictable behavior but he shrugged it off, telling her that he had a lot of business deals going on. She continued to see him sporadically and even got stood up by him again. Although it bothered Josephine tremendously, she seemed to be able to sit on her anger and keep seeing him as if nothing had happened.

Available Men Make You Anxious

You often have a difficult time handling men and understanding their thinking processes. You get very anxious waiting for a man to call after you've gone on a date or become sexually involved. You're hypersensitive to rejection and abandonment. After you become sexually involved with a man, if he is even slightly elusive or inconsistent you can become obsessive. You're afraid to get involved with an available man because the stakes are too high. You tend to get sexually involved with men right away to rid yourself of the anxiety of getting emotionally close to them. You're afraid for a man to really get to know you well because then you feel more vulnerable, yet you place yourself into even more vulnerable situations.

You Pursue Men Even When You Know They're Not Interested

You put all your energy into a "crush," hoping he'll eventually reciprocate your feelings. You spend a lot of time talking to your friends about him and looking into every thing he says or does as a possible sign that he's becoming more interested in you. This is a way of staying alone and unattached due to the low probability of a serious relationship materializing. The challenge of trying to win his love is more important to you than a real relationship or else you would seek out another man who is more available and reciprocates your feelings for him.

You Have a Hard Time Moving on from Past Relationships

You keep idealizing your ex, thinking you'll never meet a man as wonderful as him. You quickly discard new men by comparing them to your ex. You put all your energy into ruminating and obsessing about your ex rather than trying to met a new man who is available and able to meet your needs.

If you have even one of these ten behavior patterns, it will make you more vulnerable to Ambivalent Men and harder to let go of them once you've fallen. Hopefully, this discussion has helped you realize that you need to work on your thinking in order to get out of the trap you've set for yourself. Congratulations, because the first step to change is self-awareness. In future chapters I will help you eliminate any self-defeating behaviors and ways of thinking that may be contributing toward your ongoing involvement with Ambivalent Men.

NINE

UNIO MYSTICA: WHEN YOU'RE SEXUALLY HOOKED ON AN AMBIVALENT MAN

Sex is very powerful. It can be both positive and dangerous. It can be used to experience ecstatic feelings, reproduce, bond, express love, as well as violate and degrade someone. Sex is a great substitute for emotional closeness. Sometimes making love is the only way a man allows a woman to get close. Sex can also be used to escape feelings of hurt, loss, depression, emptiness, and sadness. Ironically, it could even be a way of expressing your rage and anger at a lover.

Sex connects us with all our primal feelings from when we were tiny babies being held and fed by our mothers or caretakers—our first loves. It encompasses all the senses: smell, sight, sound, taste, and touch. Except for cuddling and feeding a baby, sex may be the most intense physical closeness one human being can experience with another human being.

What Does *Unio Mystica* Mean?

"Unio mystica" means "mystic union." When used in reference to sex, it implies a sexual passion so intense that it dissolves the boundaries between the lover and the beloved. It is sexual ecstasy so profound, if two people, who were originally one person, restore their unity. Any woman who has experienced unio mystica with a man she's sexually enthralled with will tell you there is nothing else like it. Not drugs, not success, not anything. If something feels this incredible and is so full of meaning, it's going to feel like torture when it's taken away. The loss of a man's bodily contact and his physical presence alone is enough to throw a woman over the edge. No matter how psychologically healthy you are and how great your family background is, you will experience a tremendous amount of deprivation when a man you made love to is gone. It's only natural that you feel horrible and want to get back with him again. You want to be relieved of the pain of losing him and the physical intimacy you shared. However, some women can't let go of men they've had sex with no matter how hard they try, even if the man is narcissistic and cruel. They have tremendous difficulty mourning and grieving the loss of their Ambivalent Men, and moving on. For example, imagine having earth-shattering, hot sex with a man you are terribly attracted to. Afterward, your man calmly leaves and you don't know when or if you're going to see him again. When you ask him, he tells you that he'll give you a call. By now, you should recognize these as flashing warning signs of an Ambivalent Man. Would you get sexually hooked on a guy like this? Many women do.

I have a message board on which women can post their most pressing feelings, thoughts and questions about Ambivalent Men. Not surprisingly, many of the posts come from women who feel they are "hooked" on great sex with their Ambivalent Men. One such message asks: "What is the connection between having sex with an Ambivalent Man and becoming hooked on him? When I read these posts I see a common theme—once you have sex, your ability to reason goes *poof*. It is as though once the vagina becomes engaged, your brain leaves your body. You go into a trancelike state and pretty much say: 'I slept with him. It felt great. This is the person I am meant to be with, and I will see that this works out no matter what, whether he wants it or not. Even if we are not compatible, he treats me like crap, and says he doesn't see a future for us, if I see we have great sex and chemistry that's all I need to know.'"

How Does the Ambivalent Man Hook You?

Before we examine why women continue to get hooked on Ambivalent Men, first lets look at what kind of man is it that makes even the best of us vulnerable to his sexual charms.

Non-Ambivalent Men who want stable relationships will either be into the relationship or not. If they believe the sex is good they come back for more. They don't risk losing you by temporarily abandoning you. But Ambivalent Men are different. They have a way of relating that provides an eroticism that captivates women. Certainly it's not their great sexual technique because women report sometimes that they're not even good in bed! Most of the time it's not that they're well endowed or especially good-looking. Often they're not even attractive.

It is primarily because of the Ambivalent Man's unconscious ability to create a dynamic of distancing and returning to you. He knows how to disappear or hold himself aloof. When it gets to the point you may completely lose interest, he makes a return appearance only to disappoint you again. He knows intuitively the longer and more traumatizing his disappearance or disinterest the more his value goes up. Finally, he knows how to excite the wounded desperate little girl in you that hungers for love and connection to only let you down over and over, provoking deep feelings of pain and abandonment. Whenever it's played out there's always the threat of rejection and loss hovering over the sexual connection you have together.

Why Does He Do It?

Is he hostile toward women? Sometimes that's part of the reason but more often it's more out of familiarity and self-protection. This love-lost and love-returned cycle was inflicted on him by one or both of his parents when he was a little boy. It's all he knows.

By abandoning you, he is able to conquer the painful experience he associates with abandonment and hurt from his childhood. Now, as a grown man, he sacrifices the love he hungers for deep down for the pleasure and emotional safety of constantly rejecting the woman he's with. The bottom line is he'd rather play a cat-and-mouse game than take the risk of really and truly loving a woman.

Vincent, a thirty-four-year-old, strikingly handsome car salesman found it almost impossible to sustain a relationship with a woman. He was suffering from feelings of loneliness and depression despite having many people in his life. He reported that his mother suffered from bipolar disorder and was often too depressed or manic to take care of him and his brother when he was a little boy. When Vincent was six, his father decided that Vincent and his little brother should permanently live with his unmarried aunt who had no children.

When Vincent became a teenager, he realized the enormous sexual power he had over women with his Hollywood looks and boyish charm. He began to date and became very sexually active. Throughout his adult years he had many relationships with women, and was even married once, though he divorced shortly afterward.

He explained that once he decided he liked a woman, he would pursue her relentlessly until she returned his interest. He enjoyed the chase but as soon as she became at all demanding or needy in any way, he felt a compelling urge to get away from her. He didn't know why but he felt very closed in and wanted to leave. Often he would do one of his disappearing acts after a great night of passionate lovemaking. He would usually vanish from her life without an explanation and not return her phone calls.

After he had some distance and space, he would then feel lonely for the women and long to see her again. He'd surface again showing her intense interest. If she was angry for his ignoring her, he'd woo her back until she forgave him. He noticed that some women wouldn't put up with his ambivalent behavior and refused to speak with him. However, some women became even more intensely attracted to him after he contacted them again. He couldn't help but notice that the sex was much more intense with the women who enthusiastically took him back. It almost made leaving her worth it. Although he knew he was blessed with the ability to attract women to him, he still suffered with a tremendous amount of regret that he could not develop a relationship with a woman that lasted.

In therapy Vincent became more in touch with his feelings and was able to remember that he suffered tremendous anxiety about being taken from his mother when he was six. When he allowed himself to stay connected to his feelings about the woman he was currently dating rather than run away, he realized that he was anxious about getting too close to her. He was able to feel emotions like anger, intense love, envy, and hatred. He realized that up until now it was easier to just leave than to stay and deal with it. Because of his issues, Vincent struggles in his relationship with his present girlfriend. However, he prides himself for not acting out his usual pattern of vanishing. Instead he is discussing and processing his feelings about her in his therapy sessions.

Because many Ambivalent Men are struggling with feelings of abandonment and emotional deprivation they have developed behavioral traits to protect themselves from ever getting hurt again. Unfortunately, when you get involved with a man like this you are the target of the childhood issues he's struggling with. Now that you understand why you may be sexually hooked on the Ambivalent Man, it's time to explore why you voluntarily take part in his seductive dance.

Why Do You Put Up with It?

So, why do so many attractive, beautiful, smart, often successful and accomplished women put up with awful rejecting behavior for occasional intense sex? And why are others able to turn a man down no matter how great the sexual chemistry is?

There has been a great deal of academic and psychoanalytic literature written on this subject dating back to the early 1900s. One of the early psychiatrists to address this issue was Austrian psychiatrist Richard Krafft-Ebbing who said that "the instinct of feminine servitude is everywhere discernable. Subordination is a normal manifestation of female sexuality." He went on to say that for men "love is only an episode. To remain in love, women will make all concessions necessary to a male and willingly plunge herself into a deeper and deeper bondage to him." Later, Anne Reich, a world-renowned psychoanalyst and psychiatrist, treated many women who were sexually enthralled with men they were having affairs with. She found that many of the women completely idealized their men. She observed that for these women, having sex was a way of symbolically incorporating the man's characteristics they admired into themselves.

In my sessions, when women complain about being unable to let go of a man, they usually are idealizing him in some manner. They always think he's hot and sexy and that they are meant to be with him. After some discussion, they will usually break down and fess up to the fact that he's not even that good-looking and sometimes even lousy in bed. Often the guy is a major loser in other aspects of his life as well. But what they are idealizing is his lack of neediness, his ability to be so distant and smug. In some way they wish they could be like him and occasionally report feeling almost inferior next to his magnificence. If he would suddenly act needy, wanting and longing for their in return, then the spell would be broken. The sex would be downgraded to mediocre.

Are You a Masochist?

Reich did not find this dynamic in her male patients. The word "masochistic" flashed at me like a neon sign while reading her papers. Freud, the father of psychology, defined masochism as sexual excitement associated with pain and suffering. When a woman says that a man treats her "like crap" by rejecting and abandoning her between sexual encounters, isn't that mental pain and suffering entwined with sex? Maybe he's not physically hitting her while he's having sex with her, but there is always the lingering truth, whether it's expressed verbally or not, that he's emotionally hurting her over and over. Therefore, emotional pain is mixed with their sexual connection.

Whenever a woman is sexually hooked on a man who isn't good for her, the threat of abandonment and rejection almost always lingers. You'll almost always find a history of the man having left her at some point. Consistency and availability don't mix into the formula of this electrifying sex that's glorified by the women who get involved with Ambivalent Men.

At least 90 percent of women I meet with who are sexually hooked on Ambivalent Men have at least one parent who showed them some love and sporadically met their needs, but were frustrating, hurtful, or emotionally neglectful on an ongoing basis. Mixing the promise of love and emotional gratification, and at the same time deeply disappointing a little girl by not following through on that promise, is the groundwork for a woman to become a vulnerable victim to men who like playing out their ambivalence and psychological issues. These men are especially effective if they use sex as their venue to work through their emotional problems.

A woman with an ambivalent parent has similar feelings for both her parents and her Ambivalent Man. Both relationships are intense and filled with a plethora of conflicting emotions including excitement, happiness, love, anger, anguish, longing, and sadness. Women who are sexually hooked on Ambivalent Men often don't know what it's like to have a parent who adored and loved them without chaos, drama, and conflicting messages.

Women who get sexually hooked on Ambivalent Men are often degraded by being rejected, stood up, and or lied to in the process of desperately trying to hang on to them. Usually this cruel behavior is intermittent with occasional positive gratifying times the Ambivalent Man

147

throws in to keep the women hooked. After she is humiliated by his abandonment, then she has to put the energy into restoring herself so that she has the emotional strength to carry on with the other parts of her life. A repetitive cycle of being shamed and recovering starts. This degradation/recovery dynamic may have been played out with her mother or father, or both. She is recreating with a man an adult version of how her parents might have related to her This kind of destructive behavior pattern may also be the way her mother related to men (including her father).Copying her mother's behavior is a way of staying connected to her.

Replaying Ancient History

The bottom line is clinging to an Ambivalent Man, even for sexual reasons, is a way of staying attached to your dysfunctional parent/child relationship. You're recreating a piece of your childhood that you're not willing or ready to let go of yet.

Jocelyn, a divorced mother of a young son, came to see me because she felt she was sexually hooked on Donald. She met Donald, a local auto mechanic, at a neighborhood bar around a year ago. She explained that from the beginning, he never actually took her out on a date. They were basically "just sleeping together." He would usually give her a call and then go over to her apartment or she would go over to his place. He would never take her to a movie or restaurant and always called her at the last minute.

Although Donald occasionally told Jocelyn he loved her, she didn't confront him about his never wanting to do anything with her besides have sex. Instead, she preferred to think that he would eventually change. After a night of intense lovemaking, he would leave and not contact her for weeks at a time. She would try to forget about him and then he would give her a call and want to get together again. If she called him to get together he was not always available, explaining that he was busy with work or going out with the some of his buddies.

In therapy Jocelyn was able to express her feelings of humiliation caused by Donald's lack of interest in taking her places and not wanting to see her more often. She'd always rationalized to herself that he needed to sow his oats (even though he was in his thirties), and that eventually he would marry her. She openly admitted that she was totally hooked on the great sex they had together and couldn't bear thinking about giving it up.

In therapy Jocelyn spoke about her mother who was cold and emotionally unavailable to her when she was a little girl. She didn't remember her mother ever hugging her or telling her she loved her. Even as

149

an adult Jocelyn experienced her mother as being very detached and insensitive to her feelings. She thought that the intense sex filled a void in her that longed for love and closeness. Despite the work Jocelyn did in therapy she would not give up her sexual relationship with Donald and eventually stopped coming to sessions. They continue to occasionally get together for sex and have still not gone out to dinner.

You're Only Deluding Yourself

Often women like Jocelyn who get sexually hooked on Ambivalent Men have a hard time accepting the concepts I've explained in this chapter. They attribute their sexual longings to kismet and romantic chance. They keep going back for more no matter how many times their man abandons or disappoints them, because they cling to the unrealistic optimism that their Ambivalent Man will magically change and become a committed stable boyfriend or husband. They have temporary amnesia about how much the guy has hurt, humiliated, and even emotionally abused them in the past. They fixate on the hope the he'll come through for them the same way they hoped their Ambivalent parents would do. It gets to the point that their sense of reality sounds almost delusional when they're talking about him. Some of the woman are so unrealistic about their Ambivalent Man, it's hard to imagine that they are as emotionally healthy as they seem, because they often are very accomplished, with very responsible jobs and lives.

He's Not Going to Change, So Why Don't You?

I can tell you right now, from my clinical experience and years of working with women who've been caught up in these scenarios, *he's not going to change.* It just ain't gonna happen. If he's going back and forth, breaking up with you, then coming back, he's not going to do a dramatic turnaround.

So, even if you totally understand now just how dysfunctional he is, how you're traumatizing your self every time you see him, you're still wondering why you're sexually hooked on him. One of the major reason is you don't know what he's going to do next. For all you know, this could be the last time you'll be with him. Sexual intensity is always magnified by separation and loss followed by reunions and making up.

Granted, no matter how I dissect and analyze the topic, the sex is still great. However, I think you should also examine why the excitement and pleasure is more important than the grief and humiliation you experience when he distances and abandons you again and again? You need to face the reality that this kind of intense sex is self-destructive in the long run. It's physically depleting and emotionally draining from all the aggravation and drama you deal while he acts out his ambivalence issues by always disappearing after the "great merger." Deep down you know it always ends up tragically with your feelings hurt. Nothing of substance ever comes of it. A real relationship with a future and commitment will never materialize with him. Getting together with him for the intense sex may feel good momentarily, but in a larger sense, you are attaching yourself to a painful go-nowhere situation.

Have you considered all the other great feelings in life you're missing out on by remaining sexually hooked on him? Things like being part of a permanent couple, and building a life and future with someone who doesn't cause you pain and heartache? Don't the wonderful feelings that could result from these experiences with another type of man count for anything? Maybe you're better off putting your energies into finding out why you cant have unio mystica with a man who fully reciprocates your feelings and doesn't break your heart, rather than putting your energies into staying sexually hooked on an Ambivalent Man? Only you have the power to create your own happiness, and by taking control of your life and going after what truly makes you happy, you'll find that you have no need for the likes of an Ambivalent Man.

In future chapters I will teach you how to focus your energy on cultivating strong, healthy relationships.

TEN

The Desperate Woman

Eileen, an English professor, was dating Sonny for six years when she came to see me for a consultation. Sonny was a lawyer she admired and idealized. However, he never saw her on the weekends or holidays, explaining that he didn't believe in birthdays and Christmas. He told Eileen he was busy with business social functions on the weekends and never mentioned including her. Eileen was also extremely busy with her career trying to get academically published and finish up her Ph.D. Besides the limitation of their getting together, Eileen's major complaint was that sometimes Sonny would accuse Eileen of having affairs with other men. Although this was completely untrue, Eileen would become hysterical trying to get Sonny to see that the affairs were in his imagination. He would stick by his accusations and refuse to speak to her. Unable to tolerate his latest rejections, Eileen went over to Sonny's apartment and fell to her knees begging him to forgive her for something she didn't even do.

Eileen is a desperate woman. Even though she is not dependent on Sonny financially and didn't see him often, she felt she could not survive without Sonny, who obviously had very severe psychological problems.

Feeling and acting desperate is like poison when dealing with men. Desperation makes you look needy and clingy. If someone acts desperate enough he or she can look downright pathetic. This is a genderless issue. Have you ever had a man pursue you nonstop? He presents no challenge and is totally available? He calls you all day long, every day. He leaves you nothing to fantasize about, nothing to yearn for. Well, that's what it feels like when a man is relating to a desperate woman.

The Desperate Woman Quiz

Although we can all act desperate on occasion, some of us may experience feelings of desperation more frequently than others. Take the following quiz to determine if you have any tendencies of being a Desperate Woman:

1. Do you call your boyfriend more than once a day?

2. Do you need to process what's going on with your boyfriend with a friend more than once a day?

3. If you had an opportunity to go on an all-expenses-paid trip, but your relationship with your man is rocky, would you turn down the trip to not risk losing your relationship?

4. If you've just started dating a man, did you initiate getting together with him more than once this week?

5. If the man were hesitant, would you keep perusing?

6. If you've just started dating a man would you pick up the tab for him more than once in a week?

7. If a man your attracted to called you at 11 P.M. on a Saturday evening and asked you to go out right then, would you go?

8. Do you feel your life is meaningless if you're not in a relationship with a man?

9. Would you have sex with a man if he refused so use a condom?

10. Do you have sex with a man and don't bother to insist he use a condom?

- If you answered yes to two or more questions, you may have a tendency to swing in the desperate direction.

- If you answered yes to four or more questions, you probably struggle with feelings of desperation.

What Does It Mean to Act Desperate?

When you're acting desperate, you'll do anything for a man. In desperate moments, you don't care about your self-esteem, pride, or the future consequences of your actions.

Oftentimes, a woman who acts very desperate can even humiliate herself or look totally foolish—all that matters is the man's attention, love, and, most of all, that he doesn't reject her. Some women even go to the extreme of breaking the law! It's important to be on top of your feelings of desperation because they can lead to self-destructive behaviors that you may regret later on. The following are signs that you are acting desperate:

- You grovel to a man.

- You seek revenge.

- You stalk a man.

- You harass a man.

- You pursue a man who doesn't reciprocate your feelings.

Acting desperate is often triggered by an Ambivalent Man's behavior such as by his rejecting you. However, sometimes we bring it on ourselves by the way we think. Patterns of thinking in desperation can include these:

- Blaming yourself for an Ambivalent Man's behavior

- Pitying yourself

- Obsessing about him

- Not focusing on the here and now

- Idealizing him

- Thinking you'll never meet anyone as wonderful as him

What Makes a Woman Desperate?

Desperation comes from having a poor sense of your self. The world famous psychotherapist and author Rollo May explained that "'the self' is the organizing function within the individual and the function by means of which one human being can relate to another." He went on to explain that "the self is always born and grown in interpersonal relationships."

The development of your sense of your self is a reflection of your experience with your parents. If your parents had a lot of personal problems and were emotionally empty inside, they may not have had the psychological nutrients to give you so you could develop a strong sense of self. This includes parents who were too demanding, neglectful, and/or abusive.

You originally depend on your parents to develop your emotional resources which you draw on later as a grown woman. If your parents didn't provide love and attention , it prevented your sense of self from evolving to its full capacity. When your sense of self isn't strong, you end up depending on people in your environment to mirror and validate you. You need other people (especially men) to make you feel good about yourself. You're less sure of what your feelings are telling you, so you'll end up more vulnerable to Ambivalent Men acting out. You'll always blame yourself rather than see when it's their issues. You will have a hard time feeling comfortable within yourself to set boundaries and not put up with behavior you find disrespectful.

Deborah was a woman with a poor sense of self. Her mother was a very sweet woman but was also very compliant and had problems standing up for herself. Her father was pretty much withdrawn and didn't pay much attention to Deborah. As she grew older she never had much confidence in herself and also had difficulties setting boundaries. Whenever she made a decision about anything, she always needed validation from her friends and mother. By the time she was in her late twenties the problem came to a head when she moved in with her boyfriend Russell. He would ask her to do things she didn't want to do but she would comply anyway just like her mother did with her father.

One time he asked her to deliver illegal drugs to a friend of his. She had difficulty saying no and standing up to him. She enjoyed living with a man and didn't want to go back to living alone. She reluctantly did what he asked but later told him she would never do anything illegal again for him. He told her she was too square and a fuddy-duddy. The next week he stole money from her purse, but denied taking it even though it was in her wallet when she went to sleep that night. She made herself believe him even though she knew deep down he was lying. Afraid that her reluctance to stand up to Russell was turning into a dangerous situation, she came to see me for a consultation. In therapy she worked hard to build up her sense of self and get over her fear of being alone, and eventually she left Russell. When she started dating again, she became very strict about her boundaries and her believed more in her own thoughts and opinions.

Exploring Your Own Sense of Self

When you don't have a strong connection with your self you tend to concentrate more on the "other" (the Ambivalent Man, for instance). Being more focused on the Ambivalent Man can lead to feeling desperate, especially if you are afraid he's going to leave you. The following list of positive characteristics can help you determine if you have a strong sense of self:

1. Being able to express your needs regardless of the consequences

2. Being able to enjoy spending time alone

3. Feeling comfortable setting boundaries

4. Being able to leave a situation when you can see you'll get hurt

5. Feeling deserving of the best life has to offer

6. Feeling that your need to take care of yourself is more important than holding onto a man

7. Loving and liking yourself

8. Being able to say no

9. Being adequately in touch with your feelings

10. Trusting your intuition

Are you still struggling to define your sense of self? You can become more self-aware and self-connected by doing more exploring and becoming more familiar with yourself. Strengthening your sense of self is actually a lifelong process, but one you can start working on now. To begin, look over the questions below and journal the answers on a separate sheet of paper:

- Can you describe your self?

- What part of your self do you like?

- What parts of your self would you like to change?

- In what ways are you unique?

- What is your the vulnerable part of your self?

- How do you feel about your   physical self?

- What are the strongest parts of your self?

- List your accomplishments in your life?

- What would you consider your assets?

- What are your favorite leisure activities?

- What are you passionate about?

As you become more in touch with different parts of your self you'll be better equipped to stop yourself from freaking out when your Ambivalent Man starts distancing. The next time you start feeling clingy, rather than focusing on the Ambivalent Man who's provoking some of your feelings, why not focus on what you can do to soothe and strengthen yourself? You don't have to act out with your Ambivalent Man what's going on inside of you. Instead ask your self what is it that you need or want to make you feel less desperate. So the next step is becoming more of aware of your needs.

Exploring Your Needs

An important feature of having a strong sense of self is being aware of your needs and trying to get them met if possible. As I explained, if you had parents who weren't there for you or were incapable of meeting your needs, it may be hard for you as a grown women to even know what your needs are and attempt to have them met. If this describes your situation, it's a good idea to practice getting in touch with your relationship needs. For example, when I'm in a romantic relationship, this is what I need from my man:

- Reliability (calls when he says he will)
- A good listener
- Intellectually stimulating
- A good sense of humor
- A good conversationalist

What are your needs in a relationship? Write them in your journal or on a piece of paper and post them somewhere visible. Go back to them whenever you feel as though you're being jerked around by an Ambivalent Man.

Building Up Your Sense of Self

As I said before, building up your sense of self is a long process. As you work to build up your sense of self, try the following suggestions for one week and notice how much stronger   you feel:

- **Start by giving yourself massive self-acceptance.** Don't make any demands on yourself this week. Try accepting yourself exactly the way you are right now.

- **Try spending one full day of not allowing yourself one negative thought about yourself.** See how difficult that would be. Keep count of how many times your have to stop yourself. How habitual is it to be negative about yourself?

- **Don't talk to anyone who is critical for a week** (if you can help it). Hangout with and talk to only nurturing, reliable, safe people. See how that feels.

- **Treat yourself as if you were your own child.** Talk to yourself the way you might soothe a child. Stop being the dysfunctional parent you had as a child and try to be the nurturing parent you wish had a as a little girl.

- **Be responsive to all your emotional and physical needs.** Be kind and loving to yourself Ask yourself every hour: What can I do to make myself feel better? What do I need right now? Don't reprimand yourself at all, no matter what   happens during the day.

- **Have complete confidence in your decisions.** When you doubt yourself this week tell yourself you believe in your decision or action. Don't "I shoulda" "I coulda" yourself.

- **Don't be so hard on yourself.** Don't criticize yourself at all this week. Every time your pick on yourself, stop it. Don't compare yourself to others—try saying something positive and supportive instead.

- **Everyday do something special for yourself** (get a massage, get your hair done, go to a movie).

- **Develop a healthy curiosity about your personality and behavior.** When you want to act desperate or self-destructive, question yourself and don't be satisfied with simple excuses. Learn to dig into yourself, and ask yourself what you're feeling.

- **Act as if you have a strong sense of entitlement.** Claim it even if you don't mean it. Try it on for size and see how it feels.

Develop a Sense of Entitlement

A woman who has successful, fulfilling relationships with men feels entitled to be with a man who loves her and wants to share his life with her. When a man behaves or indicates in any way that he's not interested in her or a long-term relationship, she leaves. She doesn't want to waste her precious time and energy on a man who's going to play games and hurt her.

Although it sounds as if feeling entitled could imply a woman who's spoiled or stuck up, that's not the case. Developing a healthy sense of entitlement means creating a positive way of thinking and behaving that show you truly deserve and have the right to expect good treatment from a man. Despite your past and what you saw and experienced as a little girl, as a grown woman you deserve to have your needs met. You expect to be treated with respect and not be degraded and humiliated when you are relating to a man.

My sister-in-law Beth is very happily married to my brother Drew. She said that when she was dating (before she met my brother), if a man indicated in any way he wasn't interested in her, she would stop dating him. She was not into one-sided relationships. She was not scared to be alone if a man didn't meet her expectations, so she would break up with him. She always knew inside that she would meet someone new. And she eventually met my brother. She explained that when she was dating, she would not tolerate . . .

- A man who would not return her phone calls.

- A man who would just disappear and return when he felt like it on his time table.

- A man who was in any way disrespectful to her.

What do you feel entitled to in a relationship with a man? Write down five things:

1.

2.

3.

4.

5.

What will you *not* tolerate in a relationship with a man? Write down five things:

1.

2.

3.

4.

5.

Feeling the Void

Many times when a woman acts desperate, she is running away from an intense, empty feeling she gets when she is alone. This empty feeing has often been described as a panic attack, an emptiness, a void. It's even been described by many people as a "black hole." This emptiness is so overwhelming, a woman would rather tolerate a man's awful behavior than face the horror of being alone with these terrifying feelings.

However terrifying these feeling might be, this void is not real. It has nothing to do with a man, Ambivalent or otherwise. A man, no matter what or who he is, can't make up for what you didn't get from your parents. And that's exactly what the void is all about—what you didn't get emotionally from your parents. You can't change what emotional support you didn't get from your parents. However, being in a relationship with a man who meets your needs can be healing and will help repair your past. By repeatedly involving yourself with an Ambivalent Man who keeps you in a state of deprivation and emotional pain, you're just re-enacting your childhood history and retraumatizing yourself.

In order to stop feeling desperate, you must face this emptiness and darkness. How do you do that? You have to do whatever it takes to endure these feelings while you are experiencing them and do your best to move past them. As you do this more and more, you will feel yourself gaining strength.

It's important to understand that feeling something is not the same thing as acting out the feeling. So *feeling* desperate is not the same thing as *acting* desperate. You can feel anything you want and discuss and process your feelings with safe reliable people. But acting out your desperation is what leads you to trouble and self-destructive behavior.

Allison, a single forty-year-old woman, met Elias online. They had been dating for six months when he broke up with her. Allison had a difficult time getting over the breakup and found herself calling and sending e-mails to him every day. He continued to reject her, which made her even more upset and depressed.

Allison had a disastrous past when it came to dating men. Whenever she'd go through a breakup, she would have a difficult time functioning on the job and moving on with her life. In her last breakup with her boyfriend before Elias, she became so depressed she had to be hospitalized. After getting stabilized on antidepressants, she felt much better and was able to go back to work. When speaking about her past, she was able to get in touch with an intense emptiness she experienced whenever a man left her. She described it as if she were falling into a deep hole.

Upon further exploration she was able to discuss the loss of her mother, who had died of cancer when Allison was seven. Her father was a physician and worked long hours. So, after her mother's death, she was basically raised by a nanny. In therapy she was able to connect to experiencing a feeling of enormous emptiness at seven when her mother, who she loved dearly, was gone. Allison was able to realize that when a man left her, it brought up the old void she experienced as a little girl. Terrified of this horrendous painful emptiness, she'd do anything to not feel it again, including calling her ex-boyfriend a million times a day because, even though he wasn't coming back, at least speaking to him was some kind of connection.

Staying with a man who rejects you to avoid the "the void" can ultimately lead to acting desperate, just like Allison who called her ex-boyfriend all day long. By learning to live with the void, or better yet, realizing that the void has noting to do with the man but with what's inside of you, you'll be able to guard yourself against situations that may cause you to feel the void. In doing this, you won't act desperate or stay with men who treat you badly and hold no promise of future commitment.

When Allison was able to stay with the feelings of emptiness and endure them rather than desperately clinging to a man who rejected her, she realized that the feelings would eventually go away, especially when she contacted people in her support system.

Enduring the Void

The following is a list of things to do to help circumvent acting desperate when you're feeling "the void":

- **Make a connection.** It can be a pet, child, friend, therapist, or relative—anybody but your Ambivalent Man. Isolating yourself while feeling the void is the worst thing that you can do.
- **Find a safety blanket.** Look through old pictures of times that you felt good. *Do not* look at old pictures of your Ambivalent Man! Life is filled with cycles, and even the tough times will pass. By looking at photos that remind you of

happy times, you will be able to endure the void and move past the pain and into a more meaning phase of your life.

- **Get physical.** Get back into your exercise routine. Go for a walk or run. Sign up for a yoga class. Let your emotions move through your body, rather than keeping them locked inside.

- **Give thanks.** So many people report that when they look at a written list of the things they have to be grateful for, they feel immediately better. You'll see how much fuller your life is than it feels at this moment. There are so many things in life that can give you love and pleasure other than your Ambivalent Man.

- **Catch a flick.** How about that romantic comedy everyone's been talking about? Or maybe even check out a classic or two. Anything that's entertaining and distracting will help you get past the void.

- **Surf the net.** If you can't get out of the house for some reason then go on the Internet. Go to a chat room, a dating site, personal ads site, or an online bookstore. You can even check out my message board on my Web site (*www.rhondafindling.com*) and read what other women are going through, and leave them a message.

- **Find comfort in the kitchen.** Nurture yourself with your favorite food. Try something healthy and organic, or cook or bake something gourmet. Have you ever baked an apple pie from scratch using real apples? Nothing says "nurture" like a hot apple pie right from the oven. Treat yourself!

- **Be a hydro-queen.** Try out those bath salts that have been sitting in your bathroom closet since last year. Light candles for atmosphere, put on your favorite CD, and enjoy a long, relaxing soak. You'll be amazed at how your frame of mind improves when you are relaxed and taking care of yourself.

- **Pamper yourself.** Get a massage, manicure or pedicure. The safe, physical touch of these activities can be nurturing, healing, relaxing, and most of all will make you feel fabulous.

- **Go to a twelve-step program meeting.** There are twelve-step program meetings all over the world at all times of the day and night. If you believe you're going to act desperate, go to any twelve-step program meeting and connect with other people who understand how you feel.

- **Call your therapist.** If you feel that you're going to act self-destructive in the face of the void, call your therapist for an emergency crisis session.

During the times you feel the void closing in, the most important thing to remember is that you must take care of yourself and nurture yourself. It is a spiritual truth that this, too, shall pass. The worst thing you can do during the times you are feeling abandoned is to abandon *yourself.* Connection during these times is crucial, but don't connect to the Ambivalent Man! Most likely, his behavior is triggering your desperation, and contacting him will only increase the feelings that you're already trying to cope with. Instead, make an effort to connect to people and things that bring you healthy happiness, even if it means taking extra steps to do so.

One time I ended a relationship with a man I knew there was no future with, and I was in incredible pain. I knew if I saw my nieces and nephew my healing would start immediately. I literally took a cab to the airport and booked a flight down to Georgia where they live and spent a weekend bonding with my precious nieces and nephew. The minute I saw them, the void vanished. When I returned to New York the pain was still there but had greatly diminished.

Stay in Touch with Your Feelings

When you get the urge to act desperate it's of paramount importance to stay in touch with all of your feelings. Remember, you can feel them but you shouldn't act them out. Make a list of five things you can do for yourself to prevent yourself from acting out when you're feeling desperate:

1.

2.

3.

4.

5.

The Most Desperate Woman

Let's look at an example of a woman who sunk to the lowest depths of desperation—the nationally known case of Clara Harris, the dentist who was convicted of killing her adulterous husband by running him over with her Mercedes-Benz. After learning of the affair her husband was having with his lover, she said that she had been "working tirelessly to save the ten-year marriage." She quit her job so she could have sex with him three times a night, cook his favorite meals, schedule breast enhancement surgery and liposuction, go to a tanning salon, have her hair done daily, and exercise at a gym. The day after he confessed to sleeping with his lover, Clara and her husband spent an evening at a Houston airport bar going over each woman's attributes and liabilities in exact detail. Clara took notes on bar napkins which were introduced as evidence in her murder trial. According to her husband, Clara might have had "a slight edge on appearance and intelligence," but his adulterous lover was "a better listener." According to the napkins, David thought his wife "weighed too much, worked too much and dominated conversation without letting anyone else talk," while his lover was "petite with the perfect fit to sleep with, holding her all night."

By the time Clara Harris ran over her husband, she had absolutely no sense of self left. Rather than feel her rage at her husband when he humiliated her with his sadistic comparisons to his lover, she idealized him instead, desperately doing anything to hold onto him. And when she realized that she couldn't hold onto him, even though she had sacrificed herself, tragedy ensued. Why was it completely necessary for her to give up her job and mutilate her body? Why did she let herself listen to the sadistic comparisons he was telling her in the airport bar? Why couldn't she decide to divorce him and financially take him to the cleaners to compensate her for for humiliating and betraying her? That's what most women would have done.

She wallowed in her "void," terrified of losing him, acting masochistic and desperate until the moment she caught them at a hotel together. At that point, she probably realized that all her hard work of trying to make herself over to please him was for nothing. The rage that she had repressed until this point boiled over, and as a result, she tried to obliterate him and took his life.

This is the epitome of a desperate act that led not only to the tragic loss of her husband's life but the destruction of her own life as well.
What could she have done instead? A lot! She could have helped herself greatly if she could have mustered the strength to do some of these things:

- She should not have asked or listened to why her husband wanted to be with his mistress rather than her. It was not necessary for her to know.

It was painful enough just to know he was involved with another woman.

- When she saw him with the mistress she should have left, no matter how angry and painful it was.

- She should have felt and processed her pain with a therapist or a close and supportive friends.

- She should have gone into very intensive psychotherapy instead of getting breast augmentation, cooking gourmet meals, and having sex three times a night. She should have worked on reclaiming her self-esteem on her own, and not sought it out through her husband's validation

- She should have taken a look at her husband's sadism and narcissism rather than idealizing him and thinking she'd do anything to keep him.

What happened to Clara Harris can teach us just how serious acting desperate can become. Revenge, stalking groveling, and a total loss of self can never be taken lightly. Feelings of desperation that go unresolved can even lead to total self-destruction. The tools in this chapter will help you to prevent future acts of desperation.

ELEVEN

EARLY WARNING SIGNS OF AN AMBIVALENT MAN

Congratulations! You've been working hard on your self-awareness, which brings about the potential for change. However, you may still have to empower yourself by increasing your judgment skills about men. Many women complain that they get involved with men and are taken surprise by their ambivalence later. If you're really observant of your Ambivalent Man right from the beginning you'll be prepared for what's ahead, and then you won't end up feeling so victimized.

Twenty-Five Early Warning Signs

Ambivalent Men are usually on good behavior in the beginning because they're not struggling with anxiety about closeness and intimacy yet. However, their ambivalence usually starts to rear its ugly head pretty quickly.

There are twenty-five behaviors that you should be on the lookout for to identify an Ambivalent Man. If he has at least three of the signs from the start, then there's a good chance he's going to turn out to be an Ambivalent Man.

Sign 1: You Feel Jerked Around

He tells you he's going to call you at 8 P.M. but he doesn't call until 10 P.M. He says he has to wait until Wednesday to let you know about a date you both planned but doesn't call until Friday. You feel manipulated and jerked around by him.

Jenny met Renaldo at a nightclub. He was handsome and a great dancer, and she was thrilled when he called her the next night and asked her out. On Monday, an hour before he was supposed to pick her up, Renaldo cancelled, explaining something came up at his job. He called during the week to ask her out for the next weekend but said that he'd have to call her, though, to confirm. When she didn't hear from him by Saturday morning she figured he changed his mind. Then he called her that very Saturday night and asked her if she wanted to come with him to a great party. Even though she was angry that he never called that morning, she decided to give him another chance. An hour later, while she put on the finishing touches to her makeup, he called and cancelled. Infuriated, Jenny told him to never call her again, that she didn't like being "jerked around"!

Sign 2: He Takes a Long Time to Get Back to You If You Leave Him a Message

If you leave him any kind of message (e-mail or telephone) he takes a long time to respond. For instance, you send him a quick e-mail and you don't get a response for at least three days. You leave a message on his answering machine inviting him to an event and ask him to get back to you because you need to respond, and he takes more than four days to reply. You get a feeling he's got a lot more going on in his life other than developing a relationship with you, which doesn't seem to be a big priority in his life. This confuses you because he seems so into you when you spend time together.

Sign 3: He's Super Seductive

He's talks sexy and is very focused on trying to seduce you. Although you enjoy feeling so desirable it also seems as though he has a one-track mind. Sometimes he doesn't even ask you questions about yourself because he's only interested in having sex.

Sign 4: He's Unreliable

He acts out his ambivalence by being unreliable. He doesn't show up or call when he says he will. He stands you up. He's late. He's undependable.

Sign 5: He Pulls the Disappearing Act

You had a great first date and then you don't hear from him for a couple of weeks; then he seems to vanish into space. You have a great second date and again you don't hear from him for another couple of weeks. He reappears again with an excuse that he's been in bed with the flu.

Sign 6: He's Completely Unpredictable

You never know when he's going to show up or what he's going to do. It's exciting but anxiety producing. He seems as though he's not that interested and then he shows up at your job with roses. You don't know whether you're coming or going with him.

Sign 7: He's Self-Absorbed

He s selfish and very focused on himself. You try to talk to him about you but the conversation always reverts to him. He's a poor listener. He seems to have difficulties relating to other people's problems because the discussion is not about him.

Sign 8: He Wants Instant Gratification

He wants things his way and doesn't want to wait. If he asks you to go away with him and you have to find out if you can get a personal day off, he insists on knowing immediately. He's demanding and can even be infantile. It's his way or the highway.

Sign 9: He's a Mystery Man

There are things about him that don't make any sense. If you ask him, he gets defensive and continues to be elusive.

Priscilla was dating Raymond for a couple of months when she started to notice that there was something very mysterious about him. First of all, he was always screening his phone calls, which she thought was a little odd. Then he didn't want to see her on Saturday nights, just on Sundays and Sunday nights till Monday morning, so she asked him what he did on Saturdays. He claimed that he sold sweaters as a side job and went to the factories to pick them up on Saturdays and didn't come back until Sunday (although she never saw any sweaters lying around his apartment). Sometimes she'd leave him a message and he wouldn't answer her message for days, explaining he was busy or sick. It just seemed to her that he wasn't home or he had another life that he wasn't telling her about. She noticed that whenever she confronted him he would come up with an answer, and sometimes his explanations didn't jibe with each other. She eventually found out he had other parts to his life she wasn't involved with including other women and even some illegal activity.

However, some men are mysterious and elusive as a way of not getting too close. They prefer to have a piece of their life that is totally private which they don't want anyone, including a close girlfriend or wife, to be a part of.

Sign 10: He's Superficial

He's shallow, looking only on the surface of things. He easily devalues a woman once he starts to feel ambivalent, usually finding something wrong with her physical appearance.

Sign 11: He Won't Take Responsibility for His Own Behavior

He gets defensive if you point out something about the way he relates to you. He's incapable of seeing how he affects others and has poor insight into his own behavior.

Chelsea thought Gil was great until he started criticizing her. When Chelsea told Gil she felt hurt by some of the things he said to her, Gil began arguing with her telling her she was too sensitive. Then Gil promised he would call her and didn't call her. When she told him she didn't appreciate his forgetfulness he said she was too picky. After awhile she realized that Gil was unaware of the way he was pushing her away and sabotaging the relationship by his inability to take responsibility for his behavior.

Sign 12: He Still Lives with His Parents

This indicates that he may not be emotionally mature enough to have a truly adult relationship with a woman. Due to his overattachment to his parents he's likely to be ambivalent about commitment.

Sign 13: He's Married or Dating Other Women

This is a major sign of an Ambivalent Man. He avoids anxiety about closeness and true intimacy by being involved with more than one woman at a time. If you confront him he'll probably intellectualize and rationalize to you why it's okay to have multiple relationships.

Sign 14: He Talks Constantly about His Ex

He still hasn't gotten over his past relationship, and he's still not ready for a new one. It's likely he's going to start acting ambivalent pretty soon.

Sign 15: He Plays Games from the Start

He provokes arguments right from the beginning. You feel as if he's playing games. He criticizes and/or devalues you.

Sign 16: What He Says and What He Does Are Completely Different

He's sending you double messages from the beginning. He says one thing than does another. He'll tell you things he wants to do and then never follows through. For instance, he says he loves you and then doesn't call you for two weeks. He'll say you have all the qualities he's looking for in a woman but then won't want to see you the next weekend. He'll promise to take you out dancing but never does. He promises to buy a particular piece of jewelry but never buys it for you. Sometimes he's all talk and no action.

Sign 17: You Get the Distancing Lecture Immediately

On the first date he's already giving you the lecture about how he s not looking for a relationship, commitment, or anything serious. Once you hear this you know immediately he's an Ambivalent Man.

Sign 18: He's Had No or Few Relationships with Women

This is a bad sign because it means he's terrified of relationships. It's likely he'll be terrified of having one when you both start to get closer.

Sign 19: He Goes to Endless Singles Events

He's very into single's consciousness, meeting women and casual dating. This is a bad sign because it means he's rarely in relationships.

Sign 20: He Flirts but Never Asks You Out

You feel very frustrated or even teased by a man who flirts but never asks you out. He sends you double messages by appearing interested but not following through with action.

Sign 21: He Doesn't Give You His Home Phone Number

He gives you his cell number (or voice mail or beeper number) but not his home number. Any upright guy who's legitimately interested in building a relationship will simply give a woman his home phone number. If you get only a cell number, voice mail, or no number, you almost know for sure you're with an Ambivalent Man.

Sign 22: He Has a Bad Track Record with Other Women

He's had a series of relationships with dramatic, emotionally bloody endings. This is a sign of an Ambivalent Man. Listen carefully to what he says about his past because it will surely be repeated.

Hilary was dating Herb for a month when she ran into his ex-girlfriend Tiffany while they were both getting their hair highlighted in the local hair salon. Tiffany told Hilary that Herb would get her so angry with his back-and-forth behavior that she finally took all his clothes and threw them in the garbage can in her backyard and burned them. Hilary figured that Tiffany probably had psychological problems, although Herb did tell her that he'd had a lot of girlfriends in the past. After a couple of months, Herb started canceling dates and just not calling, giving Hilary the impression that he was dating other women. Since he had told Hilary that he never loved another woman so completely as her, she was devastated by his rejection. She felt as if he tricked her, pulling the wool over her eyes. Though she didn't condone it, now she understood what had prompted Tiffany's actions!

Sign 23: His Life Is Chaotic

If he has a chaotic life it's a sign that he's going to be ambivalent because a stable, quiet relationship is too anxiety inducing for him. He will need to provoke some distance to get the drama going with you.

Sign 24: He Openly Flirts with Other Women in Front of You

He provokes distance between the two of you by openly flirting with other women in front of you. He's sending you a double message that he's into you but also can be easily distracted and forget about you.

Sign 25: He Idealizes You Immediately

He starts making plans with you when he barely knows you. He acts as if he's madly in love with you. Although that can be very flattering it can also indicate that he's idealizing you, which leads to his becoming disappointed, followed by his devaluing you—classic ambivalent behavior.

Harold told Deirdre when he met her that he was in love with her. He told her she had every quality he was looking for in a woman. When they went out he complimented her on her makeup and clothes. He told her how smart she was and laughed hysterically at her jokes. He'd gaze at her while she spoke as if she were a goddess. One evening they were talking about their pasts and Deirdre mentioned that she had experimented with drugs while she was in college. Harold looked at her in shock and told her he didn't think she was that kind of person. She thought he was joking but he told her that he was very serious. As Harold got up to leave he explained that he didn't think he could see her anymore because she wasn't who he thought she was and was too disappointed. She never heard from Harold again. Harold was idealizing Deirdre, thinking she was absolutely perfect. When she disappointed him, he didn't have the emotional capacity to accept her, faults and all. He only wanted her when she was in his fantasy idealized state.

Giving Him the Third Degree

It may seem intrusive to ask him so many questions but you need to know about him to see who it is you're really dealing with. Information is power so go ahead and empower yourself. If you suspect you're dating an Ambivalent Man, get the information in the listed that follows. Although his answers can't completely guarantee that you'll know if he's going to act ambivalent, you'll have something to work with so you don't feel completely fooled and surprised later on.

Get his digits. He *has* to give you his home phone number. If he gives you only a cell number or voice mail then he's probably married or living with someone, at which point you know he's an Ambivalent Man. If you're suspicious of the phone number he does give you, check it out. If you find out it's not a regular home phone number, confront him.

Ask about his job. It's essential to know where a man works. With this information you can find out if he has a job or if he's unemployed. And while you're at it, try to find out about his past employment. If he's ambivalent about his work he'll probably be ambivalent about you, too.

Find out about his dating history. Find out if he's ever been married or had brief or long-term relationships. This is an indicator of what kind or relationship he may be capable of having with you. If he's over forty and never been married it could be a sign that he's an Ambivalent Man.

What's his family like? Ask if his parents are divorced or if they're still married. How many siblings does he have? Is he an only child? What was it like growing up in his family? How does he get along with his family now? All of this information can give you insight into his feelings and thoughts about relationships.

Find the skeletons in his closet. This may seem a little extreme, but find out if he's been in the clinker. If he has a prison record, he probably has some deep character flaws, which could indicate to you that he'd probably be ambivalent about relationships at the very least.

Get the lowdown on his education. See if he was able to commit to college, graduate school, or trade school. If he drops in and out of school it's a major sign of ambivalence.

Know his relationship goals. Sometimes men will hand-feed the answers to you. They'll come right out and tell you that they don't want to get married or they want to get married and have children. You don't want to sound too blunt, but shrewdly find out what he wants regarding love and relationships.

Start being observant from the first encounter. Of course, you want to enjoy being with him, but don't get swept away into La-La land too quickly. This is not a fairy tale. It's your life. Ask questions. You have a right to know.

Setting Limits and Boundaries

How someone responds to boundaries and limit setting tells a lot about a person. So, if he starts acting out his ambivalence from the very beginning you can set limits and boundaries. His response can tell you pretty quickly if he's an Ambivalent Man. If he keeps repeating the same behaviors, he's definitely an Ambivalent Man. Call him on it immediately if . . .

- He's late.
- He stands you up.
- He says he'll call and doesn't.
- He makes a promise and breaks it.
- He ignores you when you're out with him.

- He starts flirting with other women when he's with you.

Increasing Your Initial Intuitive Wisdom with Men

While women have the ability to see men clearly, too often they let their own neediness, longings, and hopefulness cloud their judgment. Feminist psychologists have written about how preadolescent girls have a strong sense of self and their connection to their intuition is powerful. But once a girl reaches adolescence and becomes entangled with sex and romance, her innate wisdom about boys and men becomes contaminated from societal expectations and the dating game. As an adult woman, by going back and strengthening your sense of self, you can resharpen the clarity and wisdom you innately possess and be able to detect pretty quickly if a man is an Ambivalent Man. Remember, early detection is key to nipping the problem in the bud!

TWELVE

KNOW WHEN TO HOLD 'EM: A TWLEVE-STEP PROGRAM TO DATING AN AMBIVALENT MAN

Marilyn, a forty-two-year-old divorcee with two teenage children, was dating Pete, a handsome salesman five years her junior. Having gone through a painful divorce, Pete told Marilyn he wasn't sure if he ever wanted to marry again. Although she knew from attending one of my workshops that Pete was an Ambivalent Man, she felt they connected on a lot of levels and wanted to try to have a serious relationship with him. Marilyn said he was great with her kids and she considered him a real catch. She asked me if I could give her any suggestions for trying to have a long-term relationship with an Ambivalent Man.

Can Your Ambivalent Man Sustain a Relationship?

Some Ambivalent Men have the emotional capacity to have an emotional relationship and some don't. Marilyn wanted to know how a woman could tell if a man had long-term relationship potential or if he was hopeless. Here is the list of signs that may indicate an Ambivalent Man with potential for sustaining a relationship:

- He wants to see you at least once a week.

- He gives you a phone number where you can reach him.

- You know where he lives.

- He initiates getting together at least 70 percent of the time.

- He wants to date you on the weekend, not just during the week.

- He talks about wanting a serious relationship at some point in his life.

- He wants to do things when you get together (go to a movie, out to dinner); he doesn't want to get together with you just for sex.

The Ambivalent Man Who Can't Be Salvaged

Before we further discuss how to handle an Ambivalent Man with possibilities, let's take a quick look at those who are unsalvageable. Some Ambivalent Men have even less capacity than other Ambivalent Men to have a healthy relationship. Men who are almost a total lost cause can be classified as Hopeless Ambivalent Men (as opposed to Ambivalent Men with Possibilities). Hopeless Ambivalent Men are so ambivalent they act out in a more intensive way. They are almost always unavailable, unreliable, and unpredictable, and they're just about hopeless to have a relationship with. Unfortunately, they are also often charming, engaging, fun, sexy, and seductive, which is why women even bother with them. They have that knack of making you feel desired (temporarily), making it hard to give them up even though their attention is superficial and they are not interested in meeting your needs on a deeper level. There's only one thing you can always count on a Hopeless Ambivalent Man to do: He will ultimately disappoint you. Of that you can be sure. These are the signs that you are hanging out with a Hopeless Ambivalent Man:

- He wants to get together less than once a week.
- He wants to get together during the week, never on Saturday nights.
- He rarely takes you anywhere.

- He wants to get together only for sex.

- He insists on seeing others (multiple relationships).

- He adamantly declares he doesn't want a relationship.

- He stands you up.

- He doesn't call when he says he will.

- He lies to you.

Warning! It's Not Easy Dating an Ambivalent Man with Possibilities!

If you decide to try to have a relationship with an Ambivalent Man with Possibilities, it can be stressful, emotionally depleting, and even traumatizing. You may be sacrificing some of your own needs because you'll be busy trying to endure his ambivalent behavior and not provoke even more of his ambivalence. A relationship with an Ambivalent Man won't give you a lot of time for taking care of your own needs.

You have to decide if it's a good investment of your time, energy, and mental health. After all, you're attaching to a person you'll have to detach from if things don't work out. To help you predict the odds, I'll share how a number of my clients who married Ambivalent Men handled their relationships with their Ambivalent   Men while they were dating them:

- They saw their Ambivalent Man at least once a week.

- They had ongoing contact with their Ambivalent Men throughout the week with phone calls and dates, and saw them on the weekend.

- They put a time limit on how long they would date their Ambivalent Men without a commitment of marriage or engagement.

- They were in therapy (with me) while dating their Ambivalent Men.

- They gently confronted their Ambivalent Men's ambivalence.

- They were firm when setting limits and boundaries.

- They were in love with their Ambivalent Men, although they always had doubts along the way due to their Ambivalent Men's ambivalence.

- They were successful in their careers.

- They were not financially dependent on these men, sometimes earning more than their Ambivalent Man.

A Twelve-Step Program to Dating an Ambivalent Man

If, after heading the warnings set forth in this and all previous chapters, you still feel your Ambivalent Man is what you want and need, here is a twelve-step program for dating an   Ambivalent Man.

Step 1: Have a Support System

You're going to need a support system to process your feelings when you're trying to have a relationship with an Ambivalent Man. Your support system can include relatives, friends, twelve-step program sponsors, coworkers, or a psychotherapist. The more people you have in your support network the better. This will prevent you from relying too heavily on one person, which can be draining on that individual.

You're going to need people in your life to run your thoughts by and spot-check your version of reality. They should especially help you not to personalize your Ambivalent Man's behavior. You will need them to listen to you when you have to vent your frustration, fear of loss, abandonment, or any feelings that he'll provoke by his ambivalent behavior. Your Ambivalent Man is not going to be emotionally available to work your feelings through with you. So you need to start pulling your support team together as soon as possible.

Keep the phone numbers of your support system on speed dial so you can call them when you need to speak with them as soon as you need to. Carry their phone numbers with you at all times in case you're afraid you're going to do something impulsive or self-destructive in your relationship.

When you meet new people who are supportive and helpful, add them to your

support system. And finally, be a support system for other women. It will be

healing for you to listen and offer your advice and support. You will not only

get a break from thinking about your own issues, but you'll probably learn a

lot. It's also an even exchange—you are all there for each other when you

need it.

Step 2: Don't Be Clingy

Clinging to an Ambivalent Man will definitely make him run for the

hills. When he starts acting ambivalent, your first instinct will be to cling to

him, but don't do it! If you feel needy, be sure to turn to your support system.

You'll have to work on being emotionally separate from him and his issues.

You'll have to stop yourself from getting caught up in his projections and

acting out. This may be difficult but if an Ambivalent Man is what you want,

you just have to be more self-disciplined and learn how to contain your

feelings. You could also try psychotherapy to help you process your anxiety

and feelings during this time.

It's important to keep in mind that everyone gets anxious when beginning a new relationship, even if the object of your desire is not an Ambivalent Man. This is because you're getting close and vulnerable to someone who could possibly hurt or reject you. Even though dating can be fun and exciting the beginning is stressful.

Here's what you need to do if you feel the urge to cling:

- Get in touch with the feelings his behavior is bringing up in you. What emotion or memory is being triggered? Why are you upset? Try to work through the feelings by yourself or with your support system. Just don't work them out with your Ambivalent Man.
- Distract yourself.
- Do something that makes you feel good about yourself.
- Date other men. You're better off seeing more than one man until your Ambivalent Man is less ambivalent and ready for an exclusive relationship.

- Work through your feelings by being creative (paint, write, dance, play a musical instrument).

- Do something physical (walk, work out, play tennis).

- Focus on soothing yourself.

- Do whatever it takes not to focus on him.

- Get a manicure, pedicure, or facial.

Step 3: Stop the Drama!

Don't act dramatic with your Ambivalent Man because it won't change him and it certainly won't make him act any less ambivalent. If he provokes you by distancing or acting ambivalent, stop yourself if you start to pull "a scene" to express your feelings or get his attention.

Rolanda was falling in love with John, who was from Iran and studying for his master's degree in engineering. After steadily dating for three months he took her to dinner and told her that he was engaged to a woman in Iran. He explained that he was afraid to tell her because he loved her and didn't want her to break up with him. Feeling betrayed and enraged at his withholding such important information, Rolanda ran into the bathroom and started crying hysterically. After they left the restaurant she began sobbing in his the car, asking how he could do this to her. She demanded he stop the car so she could throw up. Then she asked him to take her back to his place where they made passionate love. Afterward she argued with him all the way back to her apartment, telling him she could never see him again. Then they had sex again in her apartment. Then she started crying again and he comforted her. This scenario went on all night long.

The healthiest thing Rolanda could have done in this situation would have been to ask him to drive her home (or take a cab home by herself), tell him she needs to think about things, and that she'd be in touch. Then she could have called up all the people in her support network to help her make a clear and healthy decision about how she wanted to handle her relationship with John and if she ever wanted to see him again. She could have also cried and expressed her feelings to safe people in her support system. Carrying on in front of John like she did was pointless, since John had already betrayed her by lying to her for three months. All it did was massage his ego and make Rolanda look very desperate. In the process of acting out her hysterics, Rolanda lost some of her self-esteem, and self-control.

If you're a drama junkie you'll have to kick your addiction because it won't work with the Ambivalent Man!! Dramatic scenes will only scare away Ambivalent Men with Possibilities. Melodrama will only stir up a lot of emotions that will ultimately provoke his ambivalence and distancing, causing you to cling. So don't even get the cycle going. Process your feelings with your support system and contain your feelings of desperation no matter how powerful they are. The most important thing to remember is, contain, contain, contain!

Step 4: Understand his Past

As I suggested in the last chapter, don't be afraid to ask your Ambivalent Man questions. Learn more about him. Knowing and understanding his issues from his past (traumas in childhood and so forth) will help you to tolerate his ambivalent behavior without it taking large a toll on your sense of self. However, when he does give you information about himself do not psychoanalyze him! You can dissect his psyche with your friends, a therapist, or by yourself but not with your Ambivalent Man. If you do analyze him too much he will feel intruded upon, emotionally violated, and may get angry with you.

Learning more about your Ambivalent Man's background will also help you not to personalize all of his actions. The more information you know about him the more you will come to understand how much his ambivalent behavior is really about him and not you. Although there's nothing wrong with wanting to know more about a man your trying to build a relationship with, it helps if you can develop the skill of exploring his past without seeming intrusive.

Step 5: Set Limits and Boundaries

A boundary marks the difference between you and another person. The key to your boundaries is knowing your inner life, which includes your thoughts, feelings, choices, and needs. Boundaries tell us which behaviors are appropriate and inappropriate in a relationship. Since you're working so hard on strengthening your sense of self, it's important to figure out what are important boundaries for you in a relationship. Then you can set boundaries and limits with your Ambivalent Man. Once these boundaries are set, it is of paramount importance that you see whether or not your Ambivalent Man can honor your boundaries.

When someone acts inappropriately in a relationship by not following your set boundary, that person is violating your boundary. For instance, you tell him he can't stand you up and he stands you up. That is a boundary violation. Boundary violations can be fixed right away if the he apologizes or expresses concern about his behavior. If your Ambivalent Man gets angry or dismisses you when you confront him about his boundary violation, you have a major problem.

If he cannot honor and respect your boundaries it's just about impossible to have a healthy relationship with him. If you continue to see a man who doesn't respect your boundaries, you're displaying zero self-esteem or self-love. He'll treat you as if you were a pushover and will walk all over you. Essentially, you'll be in a relationship with a man who's not into the real you and your real needs.

Marilyn noticed that Pete had a tendency to say he was going to call at a certain time and would sometimes not call her till the next day (a definite sign of his ambivalence and dishonesty). Marilyn decided to confront Pete on this behavior. She explained to him that she found his not calling her at the time he said he would to be inconsiderate as well as rude. She said that she couldn't tolerate his lying to her and would appreciate it if he'd call when he said he would or just not say when he would call. Pete found it easier not to say when he would call if he didn't know when he could do it, or if he felt the commitment was too confining for him to make. He would tell her only when he was completely sure or it was necessary in terms of the plans they were making.

Marilyn made a list of things she would not tolerate when trying to have a relationship with Pete:

- Being stood up
- Being lied to
- Seeing her during the week (when they first start dating) and not seeing her on Saturday nights
- Ogling other women in front of her
- Disappearing for weeks at a time
- Calling to get together at the last minute
- Broken promises

- Being chronically late

- Having sex with him if he's sleeping with another woman

If you're determined to stay in a relationship with an Ambivalent Man, follow Marilyn's advice and make a list of what kind of behaviors you're not willing to put up with a relationship and be sure to stick to them. Practice telling your Ambivalent Man your boundaries by rehearsing with someone in your support system. Be firm but gentle. Don't sound too harsh, critical, or attacking. But stick to the boundaries you set, make sure you enforce them, and don't back down.

Caution: While doing this important boundary work, also be careful that you don't violate *his* boundaries as well. You can't expect him to honor your boundaries when you're stepping all over his!

Step 6: Don't Discuss Your Feelings of Love and Infatuation with Him

In the beginning you're better off expressing feelings of love for your Ambivalent Man with people in your support system rather than with the Ambivalent Man himself. He will not be able to tolerate your feelings of love and infatuation because it's too charged and scary for him. It will bring up his own longings, which he may not want to be in touch with. He may also feel obligated to share his own feelings, causing him to feel locked in and to distance from you as a result. It's best to wait for him to declare his love first. Even then, be careful. You still may be skating on thin ice. Wait until you have a more established relationship, you consider yourselves a couple, and his ambivalence has noticeably lessened.

Step 7: Let Him Initiate

Let him suggest dates, getting together, calling, or e-mailing. You can't force his feelings for you no matter how many rules and programs you implement. If his feelings of desire for you just aren't strong enough, all your work and pursuit will be a washout no matter how hard you try or how patient you are. No matter how strong the urge is, it's better not to be the initiator.

It's fine to be assertive and go after you want with men who are not ambivalent. When you first meet a man you're attracted to, go ahead and make the first move. However, with Ambivalent Men you have to be more careful. An Ambivalent Man needs to feel his longing for you. When you initiate, he can't fantasize about you because you're so available. It's important to keep in mind that if he's really into you and wants to see you, he will continue to hang in there without your prompting, regardless of his ambivalence. Even if he runs away or distances he will come back if his interest is strong enough.

If you don't initiate you'll get to see what he does when he doesn't get any prompts or reminders from you. If he doesn't want to get together or call you on his own, then you must face the reality that he's just not that interested. Even if this hurts, you must face this truth so you can strongly consider letting him go and moving on.

Alice was dating Ben, a man she had been interested in from the day he started working at her law firm. Being a successful, aggressive trial attorney, she always went after what she wanted. Even men. They seemed to appreciate her "seize the moment" attitude. She asked Ben if he wanted to go out for a drink and he enthusiastically agreed. The date went well and he asked her to a baseball game the next week. Right after the game they went out for drink at a bar in Alice's neighborhood. Over a beer they got into discussion about relationships. Ben said that he was dating a number of women and wasn't looking for anything serious right now. Alice changed the subject thinking it was way too soon to be discussing relationships. Besides, she didn't even know if she felt that way about him.

Ben acted cool to her at work the next day although she caught him gazing into her eyes at a meeting. At the annual Christmas party the next week Ben got a little tipsy and outrageously flirted with Alice, giving her the impression he was interested in her although he didn't mention their going out again. His mixed messages confused her so she decided to make the second move and ask Ben out again. They went to the movies and had a great time. The next day at work Alice got an e-mail from Ben saying that he didn't think they should date anymore. He wrote that he wasn't ready for any kind of serious relationship and it seemed to him that she was looking for that with him. Alice was angry that she had initiated the second date because he was obviously arrogant as well as ambivalent. She was infuriated that he assumed she wanted a relationship with him, claiming that he was the disinterested party, when he was sending her signals at the Christmas party and the staff meeting. She thought that if she had only waited for him to ask her out, he would have had to assume responsibility for his own feelings rather than project them onto her. She swore to her best friends that she would never make a move on one of these mixed-message Ambivalent Men ever again!

Step 8: Balance Being Emotionally Separate with Being Available

Striking a balance between being emotionally separate and being available is a challenging task but totally doable. Keep some part of yourself completely off limits to him. Yes, I'm saying be mysterious in a way, but unfortunately that's how people fall in love. You're probably the same way. If a man you adored was in your face 24/7 pushing the relationship down your throat, do you really think you could fall in love with him? Isn't it his distancing and having that small, off-limits, emotional space that keeps you intrigued and makes you want him more? So keep a part of yourself emotionally separate. Do not always focus on him and the relationship. Here are some suggestions to help you stay emotionally separate:

- Don't express all of your feelings to him at once. Take it slow.
- Don't tell him everything about yourself right away. Hold some of yourself back. This is not game playing or playing hard to get.

It's just taking care of yourself so you don't make yourself too vulnerable and then get hurt.

- Continue dating other men until he wants to make a commitment.

- Stay focused on other things besides him. Don't give up your friends, hobbies, or activities to make room for him in your life.

- Don't let yourself get so preoccupied with him that you can't accomplish your daily tasks and goals.

- Keep in mind that he may not come through for you; keep your options open.

- Do whatever it takes not to think about him all the time.

Although it may sound like a contradiction, you must also work on keeping yourself available both physically and emotionally. This doesn't mean sacrificing yourself—it just means being open to a situation. When he asks you out and you dig the guy, go out with him. Don't purposely play hard to get. The only men who like being rejected and put off are men who are masochistic and have very low self-esteem.

If you turn men down for dates or don't return their phone calls, most men will get frustrated and stop calling. They'll just disappear. Then you'll be wondering what happened and why it didn't work out. Make yourself available to dates you feel good about, like going out to social events, restaurants, parties, movies, plays—any kind of get-together that supports the development and growth of a relationship. Do not play into impulsive encounters on his part so he can get sexually gratified.

Step 9: Get Him in Touch with His Feelings

Be totally emotionally present when he's talking to you. Pay absolute attention. This kind of active listening will help him feel safe and loved. It's the very attention he either had or yearned for when he was a little boy. He will experience a safety, which will help him connect with his feelings. When he does get in touch with his emotions, do not make fun of him, analyze him, criticize him, or attack him in any way. He will get defensive and immediately disconnect. You have no control over what he does after he gets in touch with his feelings. You can only hope for the best at that point. So remember:

215

- Reflect what you hear him saying so he feels heard.

- Don't switch the subject back to you when you're listening to him.

- Show true compassion and empathy.

- Work on increasing your listening skills.

- Try not to give advice unless he specifically asks for it.

- Ask him questions, but don't be intrusive.

- Don't cut him off when he's talking.

- Try not to bring everything he says back to "the relationship."

- Don't psychoanalyze him. However, if you do see a connection between something he's talking about and a psychological issue he's mentioned, you can gently let him know your observation. However, try to do this without being intrusive.

For instance, Sybil was listening to her boyfriend go on and on about how his boss was criticizing him. Although she showed him empathy about how horrible it is to be criticized by his boss, she remembered that he was complaining just last Sunday about how his father used to be very critical. When she pointed this out to her boyfriend, he was grateful for the connection, which actually helped him not be so upset! Not only did her observation help him get in touch with his feelings but it served as a model for him to help Sybil as well. A week later when Sybil got all bent out of shape when he asked her not to leave her things scattered all over his apartment, he pointed out to Sybil that her own sensitivity to his request may be a reaction to her mother's demand for extreme neatness when she was a child, which she complained about frequently. This new process they developed to help psychologically enlighten each other has helped deepen their intimacy with each other.

Step 10: Start Confronting His Ambivalence When You See It's Sabotaging the Relationship

If you're dating steadily more than twice a week and see that you're headed toward a committed, exclusive relationship, you can start gently confronting him about his ambivalence. You can do this by telling him how you feel about his behavior. Always talk about your experience resulting from his behavior so he can't say that it's not true because it's your truth. It's your reality. He can't argue that you don't feel what you feel.

For instance, he takes you out and starts acting cold and distant to you. You can tell him: "I feel hurt you when you act cold and distant." If he's responsive to your needs and feelings you can go a step further and ask him why he thinks he acts cold and distant. If he has the capacity for insight he may actually become aware of his own feelings and not only change the way he behaves with you but possibly even feel better! The five no-no's when confronting an Ambivalent Man are . . .

1.   Don't attack him.

2.   Don't criticize him.

3.   Don't analyze him.

4.   Don't ridicule him.

5.   Don't make fun of him.

Step 11: See If You Can Get Him into Therapy

If you can get him into therapy it will help a lot. He will have more insight into himself and will *feel* his ambivalence rather than *act it out.* You can make this suggestion only if you're in therapy yourself and the relationship is getting serious. Otherwise it can be heard as critical, intrusive, bossy, and insulting. Couples counseling is another good suggestion you can consider for the two of you. Couples workshops are also helpful and even less threatening because you're not the only couple working on your issues with a therapist.

Step 12: Keep an Open Mind about the Outcome with Your Ambivalent Man

There are no guarantees that your Ambivalent Man is going to come through for you. Some of my clients have actually married their Ambivalent Men and are happy. Some of my clients' Ambivalent Men took off after they dated for only a month! You can't predict how these things are going to turn out. Some Ambivalent Men do eventually march down the aisle and then act ambivalent in the marriage (have affairs outside the marriage, act cold and distant, become workaholics). So, even if you do legally capture your Ambivalent Man there's no guarantee that he's going to be different in a marriage, and you could end up wishing that your prayers weren't answered after all!

THIRTEEN

KNOW WHEN TO FOLD 'EM: WHEN IT'S TIME TO LEAVE YOUR AMBIVALENT MAN

Tina, an attractive divorced woman in her thirties was dating Brad on and off for three years. Although Tina dated other men, she never met anyone she loved as much as Brad. However, he made it clear from the beginning that he was dating other women and didn't know if he ever wanted to get married. Tina decided that she would rather see Brad occasionally on his terms then not see him at all.

When Tina's mother passed away, she called Brad for support and emotional comfort but he was not always available. After mourning the death of her mother Tina decided that her relationship with Brad was no longer working for her and came to see me for a consultation. She explained that she wanted a deeper more committed relationship and thought that Brad was not the man for the job. She asked me to help her determine when it was time to throw the towel in and leave him.

Are you at the crossroads of your relationship with an Ambivalent Man? Are you having a difficult time deciding when it's time to give your Ambivalent Man the boot? Women who find happiness, whether they're alone or with a man, have honed the skill of knowing when it's time to leave a relationship that's going nowhere or is emotionally unhealthy. They don't spend years waiting for a man who's pretty much hopeless to come through for them.

Letting go can be an excruciating process because you're giving up the hope that what you longed for with your Ambivalent Man can ever materialize. You're saying goodbye to even the possibility. Sometimes it hurts just knowing that you spent a lot of time and energy on a man without a return on your investment. It's almost synonymous to a gambler deciding whether to walk away from the blackjack table after losing thousands of dollars or continue to gamble to win back her losses while she's risking her house and life savings.

When Is the Right Time?

There's no getting around it. Detaching from someone you care about is hard work. As humans, we are wired to bond and attach. That's why knowing when to detach from your Ambivalent Man is such a hard call to make. Goodbyes are painful. However, if you're tired of the games and you're ready to have your needs met instead of ignored, then you may be ready to leave your Ambivalent Man and put your energies into something more positive. But how can you know for sure?

In the next few pages I give you fifteen tips to help assist you in your self-examination of whether or not you should leave your Ambivalent Man.

Tip 1: Be Authentic

- During this decision-making process, you need to be brutally honest with yourself. Try to look at the situation realistically. Do not get defensive. Start by seeing if you're using the following defense mechanisms when coping with your current situation with your Ambivalent Man:

- **Denial.** Are you denying the truth to yourself about you Ambivalent Man or your relationship with him? For instance, Tina denied to herself the reality that Brad was dating other women from the beginning and that he didn't want to get married.

- **Rationalization.** Do you rationalize and make excuses about your Ambivalent Man's behavior to make yourself feel better rather than face cold hard reality? Tina would tell herself that dating a lot of women is what men do because they need to sow their oats. She convinced herself that Brad's actions were "normal" in a committed relationship. However, deep down she knew that lots of men are exclusive from the beginning and don't need multiple relationships when they're dating a woman for several years.

- **Magical thinking.** Do you think your relationship with your Ambivalent Man is going to miraculously change almost as if by magic? Tina let magical thinking take over. She always thought that, even though Brad saw her only occasionally, he would eventually want to get engaged, despite the fact that he never showed any signs of escalating their casual relationship.

Tip 2: Ask Your Support Network

Ask people in your support network their opinions of whether you should leave your Ambivalent Man or stay. Be sure to have a variety of people to turn to in your support network so you're not too draining on one person. Here are a few ways for you to get honest answers:

- Don't be defensive.

- Tell them to be really honest with you.

- Listen carefully to what they have to say.

- Don't just use them as a sounding board. Ask them what's going on in their lives, too.

Tip 3: Make Sure There's an Even Energy Exchange

If you're doing most of the work, you're in a one-sided relationship. If you're putting in most of the energy for more than a year with no positive results, then it's probably high time you threw in the towel. If the effort between the two of you is split more than 60/40, that's a bad sign because eventually the split will probably spill over to 65/35, 75/25, or worse.

Cecilia was absolutely crazy about Jimmy, who she was seeing occasionally. He'd call her once in a while to get together for dinner. Afterwards they'd usually go back to her place, where they'd spend the night together. When the holidays rolled around, Cecilia got Jimmy Christmas presents. She was devastated when he got her only a card. Jimmy never seemed to want to see her more often but Cecilia kept pursing him.

Cecilia came to my support group where she realized that she was doing most of the work in the relationship. When he finally called her after three weeks, she told him that he didn't seem invested in the relationship and decided that she didn't want to see him anymore. Jimmy called her again a few months later but at that point she had moved onto another relationship with a man who was much more available and interested in her.

Tip 4: Don't Be Influenced by Your Past

Are you staying in a relationship that is a re-enactment of a dysfunctional relationship from your childhood? If you haven't figured it out by now, repeating actions and decisions from previous unhealthy relationships is the kiss of death for your self-esteem and personal happiness. If you find yourself repeating these patterns again and again, you must continue to do more work on yourself. Once you are able to recover from your past wounds, you may find that you want a different kind of relationship with a man. By continuing to work on yourself, you will eventually be able to make this decision from an emotionally healthy place.

Irma was struggling with her decision about leaving Jose. She knew that the relationship had a lot of problems but she kept hanging in there. She was mostly concerned about his inability to stay monogamous. She knew that Jose would occasionally have flings with other women which she continually overlooked. When she came to my support group she realized that she was repeating the same kind of relationship her mother had with her father. Her mother was very tolerant of her father seeing other women while he was married to her. Irma was able to experience her anger at both of her parents for the treatment her mother tolerated from her father. After working through her feelings about her parents' relationship she decided that she would not tolerate Jose's behavior anymore, and left him.

Tip 5: Make Sure He Meets Your Needs

Make a list of five of your most essential needs you would like met by the man in your life. Ask yourself if he's meeting them. Here is Tina's list:

1.   A marriage partner

2.   Ongoing companionship

3.   Passionate sexual relationship

4.   Someone to help me with finances (she was raising two children on her own)

5.   Intellectual stimulation

Brad was meeting only two of Tina's needs. She found him intellectually stimulating and a passionate lover. However, he was never going to marry her or become an ongoing partner or companion, which she felt was her most crucial need. So she decided to end her relationship with Brad.

If he's not meeting at least three of your most important needs, you should very strongly consider dumping him.

Tip 6: Ask Yourself If He Honors Your Limits and Boundaries

Is it a constant struggle to set boundaries with your Ambivalent Man? Does he try to make you feel guilty so you will change your boundaries? Bottom line is if he can't respect your boundaries and limits, his ability to relate to another human being is very poor and he's a bad candidate for a relationship. Tina told Brad to ask her out a few days ahead of time but he always called at the last minute. Desperate to spend time with him, she often agreed to spend time him anyway despite his inability to honor her limits and boundaries.

Tip 7: Ask Yourself How Much Pain You're Willing to Tolerate

Be completely honest with yourself regarding how much pain he causes you. If the relationship is more than 25 percent heartache, you need to seriously consider leaving him. Although some people can put up with more than others, you need to examine why you tolerate so much pain. Maybe you need to do more healing work on yourself.

Tina was able to overlook her problems with Brad until the reality of him to seeing other women and never committing to her became too painful to face. At that point she made a decision to begin psychotherapy to explore why she would stay in a relationship that brings her more pain rather than happiness. While in therapy she decided that she no longer wanted to endure so much grief and heartache just to be in a relationship with a man, even if they did have some good times together, including passionate, electrifying sex.

In evaluating your situation, you must decide how much you are willing to put up with—if it's too painful, it's probably time to walk away.

Tip 8: Ask Yourself What You Get Out of the Relationship

If he's a lot of aggravation, has tons of issues, and is basically inappropriate for you, then maybe its time to call it quits. Here are some questions to ask yourself about what you're getting out of the relationship:

- Do you both communicate well?
- Do you feel comfortable with him?
- Does he validate you?

- Is he cooperative?

- Is he understanding?

- Is he reliable?

- Is he affectionate?

- Does he build up your confidence or make you feel worse about yourself?

- Do you trust him?

- Do you feel as if he loves you?

- Does he pay attention to you when you are speaking?

- Does he make you feel as though your opinions matter to him?

- Does he make you feel hopeful?

- Is he consistent?

- Is he nurturing?

- Does he listen well?

- Do you share similar views on relationships? Marriage?

- Is he a good lover?

- Does he help out financially or are you supporting him?

- Is he generous?

If, after going over the list, you feel that he contributes to your life, perhaps you should stay with him. If it looks as if he's depleting and not adding to your life, then maybe you should leave.

Tina claimed she had great chemistry with Brad, intellectually stimulating discussions, and she loved dancing with him. However, he wasn't giving her the companionship and future she longed for. Realizing how little she got from him made it easier for her to make her final decision to leave.

Tip 9: Ask Yourself If He's Emotionally Healthy

Be honest with yourself about his emotional health. If you know he has a history of psychiatric problems or drug problems then you may be taking on too much. If he acts inappropriate, maybe he just doesn't have the emotional health to sustain a relationship. Try to be objective when you evaluate this answer. Ask your support network for their objective opinions.

Marian had been dating James for a year. Although he was a great boyfriend, he kept stalling her about making a commitment and getting engaged. Part of her was tired of waiting but after talking about it with some friends, she realized that he was under a great deal of stress from finishing medical school and trying to land an internship in a prestigious hospital. She realized that although he was acting ambivalent about the future he was basically one of the most together, loving guys she'd ever known. She made the decision to give him more time.

Suzanne, however, had a different experience. She was dating Gary who was great fun to be with but totally unreliable. When she found out he was using drugs again (he had been in rehab before they met), she realized that was why he had been occasionally standing her up. He quit the drugs but then started acting ambivalent about their relationship. She thought that with his history of going in and out of rehab he was a poor choice to invest any more time in and broke up with him.

Tip 10: Make a List of Pros and Cons

Make an actual list of his good and bad points—what he's offering you and how he's depleting you—then add it up. If the negative out weighs the positive, let him go. If the positive outweighs the negative, then maybe he's a keeper.

Penny was dating Joe, who was definitely an Ambivalent Man. He'd get really into Penny and then he'd distance himself from her. Part of her wanted to break it off because she was looking for a serious relationship, but she had a good time with him. When she couldn't figure out what to do about the situation, she made a list of pros and cons to help her figure it out. Take a look at Penny's pros and cons, then make a list of your own.

Penny's list of pros include these plusses:

- Good companion
- Good conversationalist
- Funny
- Likes spending a lot of time with me
- Great lover
- He's a hairdresser, so he blows dry my hair after I take a shower almost every time he stays over (he gets three extra points for that one)
- Laid-back personality
- Not demanding
- Not critical

- Supportive to my career

Penny's list of cons include these minuses:

- Doesn't earn a good living

- Not ambitious

- Bad track record with relationships

- Drug problem in the past

- Much less educated than me

- Family thinks I can do better

- Has a chaotic lifestyle

Despite the rough patches, Penny felt that the pros outweighed the cons, so she decided to give the relationship another three months to see how things develop.

Tip 11: Set a Time Limit

How much time are you willing to wait for your Ambivalent Man to come through for you? If you want to get married and he's not ready to make a commitment, how much time will you give him? A year? A lifetime? Try to determine what's a reasonable amount of time for you. Though this may differ from person to person, a year is generally enough time for a man to decide if he wants to commit to a woman.

However, the waiting time is also determined by age and what your needs are. A woman in her twenties has more time to gamble because her biological clock hasn't started ticking yet. But a woman who's in her mid-thirties may not want to wait too long if she wants to have a family. A woman who's forty and doesn't want children can be more relaxed with time. Also, if a woman believes an Ambivalent Man has great potential, is basically a wonderful boyfriend, and is an exceptional catch, she may be inclined to give him more leeway.

Tip 12: Get Those Priorities Straight!

Be honest with yourself about what you want. Do you want a boyfriend who sees you exclusively? Do you want to get married? Do you want chemistry and passionate lovemaking even if it's sporadic and noncommittal?

Everyone's needs and wants are different. Just be strong in your convictions. If you've set priorities that you want in a partner and he can't provide for you, then you should get out of the relationship. For example, if you're yearning for exclusivity, but you're getting only passionate lovemaking when he finally gets around to calling you, then you've neglected your priorities.

Tip 13: Be Honest with Yourself

What are the real chances he'll ever change? Before you make your final decision about whether you should leave, you can confront your Ambivalent Man (calmly!) on his trying to work on issues that are bothering you. See how he reacts to your questions. Is he considerate or defensive? Does he honestly listen to what you have to say, or does he make excuses for his behavior? Do you believe that he has the capacity for change and growth? Ask yourself these questions to find out:

- Is he capable of owning up when he's acted in a hurtful or destructive way?

- Is he capable of admitting he has a problem?

- Does he exhibit self-awareness about his ambivalence?

- Is he in denial about how he   treats you and the relationship?

- Is he willing to listen to your concerns?

- Is he willing to look inside himself to further examine the problem?

- Does he have the capacity for insight?

If your Ambivalent Man claims he'd like to work on changing, that's wonderful. However, you can't just let him off that easily. You'll need to be on the lookout for concrete evidence of change from him. For instance . . .

- Have you seen concrete evidence of his attempts to change? Is he calling when he says he will? Is he listening to your concerns?

- How long has he been promising to change? Has he actually made progress?

- Are you hearing a lot of talk yet seeing no real action?

Look at these questions carefully. Is he actually making an effort, or is he up to his old tricks again? Determining whether there's enough there to work with can help you evaluate if you want to leave your Ambivalent Man or stay.

Tip 14: Look into the Future

Your answers to the following questions about your future should give you more insight into whether you should leave your Ambivalent Man. Look into your future as though you were looking into a crystal ball. How do your decisions now affect your life five years from now? Try to get into a relaxed, meditative state of mind. Close your eyes and contemplate:

- Envision your life five years from now if you stay with your Ambivalent Man. Do you believe you will be happy you stayed with him, despite his unwillingness to meet your needs? Who are the men you will not meet if you continue to stay with your Ambivalent Man? Try to visualize the possible opportunities that will pass you by (men, career, and more) if you stay with your Ambivalent Man.

- Envision your life five years from now if you were to leave your Ambivalent Man today. Imagine the possibilities that await you—a lasting love, new friends and opportunities. Let whatever you see in the future give you the information to help you to determine whether you should leave or stay with your Ambivalent Man.

Tip 15: Examine Your Symptoms

When a relationship isn't healthy, you may develop the following emotional, behavioral, or physical symptoms as a result. If you have more than two symptoms from each category then its very likely your relationship with your Ambivalent Man is causing you too much stress and you should strongly consider leaving.

Let's examine your emotional symptoms. Do you feel . . .

- Manipulated?
- Sad?
- Depressed?
- Angry?
- Hurt?
- Confused?
- Unsupported?
- Used?
- Suicidal?
- Helpless?

What are your behavioral symptoms? Do any of these describe you?

- You're preoccupied with thoughts of him.

- Your life is becoming unmanageable.

- You're taking drugs.

- You're drinking.

- You're overeating.

- You can't eat.

- You're highly anxious.

- You're not taking care of your appearance.

- You're crying all of the time.

- You're overspending.

- You're spending all of your money on therapy.

- You're smoking too much.

- You're not spending as much time with your kids.

- You're oversleeping.

- You have insomnia.

- You don't go anywhere, waiting for him to go call or come over.

- You're feeling chronically depressed.
- You can't concentrate on the job.

And finally, do you have any of these physical symptoms?

- Your stomach is in knots.
- You're tense.
- Your heart is racing.
- Your shoulders are always hunched over.
- You're exhausted.
- You feel drained.
- You're chronically sick.
- You get headaches.
- You have chronic stomach problems.

Like a Moth to the Flame

In order to remedy your situation with your Ambivalent Man, you need to examine your own motivations for being with him and enduring his ambivalence. Often, your reasons for staying with him are as psychologically complex as his reasons for being the way he is. Why do you want to stay with your Ambivalent Man?

I'm Afraid of Being Alone

If you're staying with him because you're afraid of being alone, you need to go back to Chapter 10 and work on your self-development a bit more. Once you are comfortable with yourself, you will be much better equipped to deal with whatever your relationship with your Ambivalent Man might bring. You need to work on increasing your independence so you don't feel that you can't emotionally survive without him. If you are financially dependent on him then you need to see what you can do to become more economically resourceful.

I Won't Meet Anyone Else

In this day and age, women meet men in a variety of situations. Many of the women I see in my practice who are determined to let go of their past relationships always meets someone new. It may not happen in a day or a week, but it will happen. You've just got to be open to the possibility.

Thinking there will never be another man in your life except for your ex-Ambivalent Man is totally unrealistic, self-sabotaging, and even masochistic.

I Love Him

Remember what Tina Turner asked about love? "What's Love Got to Do with It?" Women who are in unhappy, unsatisfying relationships with men say that they stay because "they love him," even though their men demoralize, reject, betray, or abuse them.

You need to explore what love means to you. Is yours the erotic love from Chapter 9? Is it dependency? Is it a road back to the great love of you had for your mother and father? If your Ambivalent Man is not making you happy and you are considering leaving him, you need to reevaluate what you mean by "you love him." Those words are important, so don't abuse them by using them to explain why you stay in a relationship that is not meeting your needs.

He Loves Me

It's wonderful to hear a man you're attracted to tell you he loves you, but you need to be mindful of his unloving behaviors. Try to be more realistic than romantic right now. Even if he says he loves you, is he really capable of love? Does he have the capacity to love you in a mature adult way, caring for your needs and wants? Or does he love you in the way a young child loves a parent? In other words, does he love you for gratifying his sexual and basic needs, but not with the enduring kind of love that makes you feel safe?

I'm a Victim

You are *not* a victim. If you waste years on a man who repeatedly hurts you or can't commit, you have to take the power into your hands and leave him. If you've been seduced into a situation that is not what you thought it would be, then leave. Empower yourself by making a decision and acting on it (I'll talk more about that in the next chapter). Use the support of your friends, support groups, twelve-step programs, books, your support network, or a psychotherapist. Whatever it takes. If you decide to stay in an unhealthy situation that depletes you rather than supports you, after awhile you have no one to blame but yourself. Remember, you are not a victim.

FOURTEEN

HOW TO STOP FALLING FOR AMBIVALENT

MEN

Things did not go so well for Marilyn (in Chapter 12). She tried the twelve-step program for dating Ambivalent Men, but Pete decided he just wasn't ready for a committed, exclusive relationship. Marilyn wanted to make changes in her life by getting involved with a different kind of man. But Pete was the sixth Ambivalent Man Marilyn had dated in a year!

So, you want a man who likes you and respects you, and you're tired of playing ambivalent games. Then how do you stop falling for Ambivalent Men? This is a very good question, indeed, and the answer, unfortunately, is not cut-and-dry. I'm going to be up front and say that I'm not one of those self-help authors who will tell you that if you read my book you're going to miraculously stop being attracted to Ambivalent Men. My book is meant to act as a guide as you make positive   changes to your life.

It may be your wiring that makes you attracted to your type of Ambivalent Men. It may be some deep-rooted unconscious reason that will take years in psychoanalysis for you to unravel. Maybe it's even genes or pheromones. It may be a human propensity for women to be attracted to bad boys who are more primitive in the sense of aggression and seduction skills, or maybe you just dig guys who have the ability to create distance. However, do not give up hope. By taking the following steps, you can start chiseling away at your tendency to fall for Ambivalent Men.

Stop Idealizing Ambivalent Men

He's not your higher power. He has positive and negative qualities just like anyone else. You are not lucky to be with him—he's lucky to be with you. Stop beating yourself up for the relationship not working out. You need to knock your Ambivalent Man off the pedestal you've perched him on. Stop making him larger than life and explore your dating options. It's important to give non-Ambivalent Men a chance. You'll be pleased when you find out they can possibly provide an even richer experience than those you encountered with Ambivalent Men.

Here are some reasons you continue to believe that no other man can measure up to how wonderful an Ambivalent Man is:

- It's an excuse for you not to have a more real relationship with a man who is available.
- You're afraid to face your anger at him.
- You'd rather control the situation by thinking he's perfect and it's entirely your fault.
- You're still holding onto your childhood relationship with your parents when you thought there was no one better than your mother and father. You idealized them and now you idealize your Ambivalent Man.

If you were to look at his bad points, you'd see how he totally contributed to things not working out and there's absolutely nothing you could have done to control it. It's just how life is. Now it's time to get out of the rut and stop idealizing Ambivalent Men.

Stop Devaluing Men

I've heard women put down men and make fun of them for being ugly, bald, fat, poor, unsuccessful, too nice, a bad dresser, nerdy, a bad dancer, not cool, and/or a pushover. These women are the very same women who complain about men objectifying women, being too shallow, and not appreciating them for their inner qualities. The men you devalue may have the very qualities you can't find in the Ambivalent Man who jerks you around and doesn't appreciate you.

Loretta and Amy were both having a hard time getting over the Ambivalent Men they had broken up with. They went out every Sunday for brunch to discuss how they were doing in the romance department. Loretta noticed that sometimes they would actually become vicious when making fun of men who were pursuing them. Loretta thought that maybe she should stop devaluing men she wasn't so attracted to and give them more of a chance. She tried dating two men that she made jokes about with Amy. She didn't fall in love with either of them but one became a dear friend, and she had a great time with the second man even though she still didn't feel any chemistry for him. Loretta decided that she was no longer going to devalue men because she found that it stood in the way of connecting with new men and letting go of her ex–Ambivalent Man.

Let Go of Your Past Relationships with Your Parents

Remember, if you had a mother or father who was dysfunctional in any way, you're re-enacting your childhood relationships by being with a man who frustrates, abandons, or hurts you in the same way. So work on letting go of the ancient mother and father that you still carry by not engaging with men who have the same issues as your parents. If you still live at home with your folks, maybe it's time you moved out. If they're giving you money, maybe you need to become more financially independent. Do whatever it takes to stop being a victim of your past.

Here are some techniques to help you move on from the past experiences and look forward to the new things to come:

- Write a letter to which ever family member you feel has caused you to have issues about men. Don't put any pressure on yourself to mail the letter—just writing it can be a healing experience. If you like, you can even mail the letter to a person in your support system who understands the kind of emotional work you are trying to do.

- Tell your story of your relationship with your parents to a safe person. Sometimes getting the story out about your life can make you feel better and is healing.

- Work through your feelings about your parents creatively. Write a short story, a poem, a song. Dance, paint, anything to express your feelings.

- Release your anger physically. Take a kickboxing class, go running, work out, move those emotions through your body.

- Have make-believe conversations with your parents. Talk to them as if they were present. You can even use the Gestalt therapy technique of talking to an empty chair, pretending your parents are sitting there and you're telling them whatever you need to get off your chest.

Just get out those emotions that are stuck and holding you back from having the kind of relationship with a man that you feel would meet your needs. If this process is too difficult for you to do on your own, then get the additional support of professional help.

Mourn Your Teenage Years

Are you attracted to men who are immature but loads of fun? An adult version of a boyfriend you would have died to have when you were fourteen or sixteen? If you didn't have a teenage romance because of weight problems, illness, disability, moving to another school, a divorce, lack of friends, or other circumstances, you may be dating adolescent men to make up for the social deprivation you experienced as a teenager. However, this kind of man you feel temporarily good with doesn't necessarily emotionally have what it takes to meet your needs as an adult woman. Having a lonely and isolating adolescence can be a traumatizing experience. You need to grieve for the happy adolescence you didn't have, so that you don't act out your issues by choosing immature Ambivalent Men.

You may also have an idealized prototype of a teenage boy you wanted to date but didn't. You may still have this teenage male image in your adult life and let it serve as your male love model. Or maybe you're doing this to recreate the intensity of teenage love you once experienced or discover it for the first time Unfortunately, the character traits in your adolescent male love model may not be the character traits you need for a mature, committed, adult relationship.

Broaden Your Horizons

One of the reasons women stay stuck on Ambivalent Men is they have so few men to choose from. You can empower yourself by widening the pool of candidates. You can start this process by taking a look at some of your ideas about "men selection" which may be too rigid and out of date. Women who are successfully finding love today are becoming more open-minded. They're exploring new territories, taking different avenues, and going outside their social circles. For instance, would you consider dating . . .

- Men outside of your religion?
- Men outside of your race?
- Men from a foreign country?
- Men from another culture?
- Men with children?
- Men who make less money than you?
- Men who are less successful than you?
- Men who are older?

- Men who are younger?

- Men who have different interests than you?

- Men with different socioeconomic backgrounds?

- Men with different family backgrounds?

Step out of the box. Go for it. Grow, challenge yourself, and experiment.

Lose Your Blueprint!

Some women have an actual blueprint of the kind of man they're looking for. They get stuck on their Ambivalent Man because it's hard to find another man with the same blueprint, who is available and into them. Forget the blueprint! Why don't you try to change and be more flexible? For instance, do the men you date have to have . . .

- A certain amount of money?

- A certain income?

- A certain amount of education?

- A certain look?

- A certain style?

- A certain job or career?

- Certain interests?

One example of inflexibility is a single woman in her thirties who isn't willing to date men who are divorced and/or widowed. To stick to the notion of having to be with a man who never married is unrealistic and impractical at that age or older. Your chances of meeting a man who is willing to have a long-term relationship and marry are probably *better* if he is divorced or widowed with kids. He actually committed to a woman at some point, unlike the bachelor who has no responsibilities and has never even walked down the aisle.

So, let go of some of that old-fashioned rigid advice that's been handed down to you from generations past. It's better to have an open mind about finding love. By believing there is only one man for you, you are limiting yourself. There are probably many possible loves out there, but you have to give men outside your blueprint a chance. You may have to stop comparing men to your ideal fantasy man. You need to have a more open attitude. Then you will have more men available to you to select from.

Play the Numbers Game

If you want to stop falling for Ambivalent Men, go out there and meet *lots* of men. Besides, this will get you away from staying focused on Ambivalent Men who aren't meeting your needs. It'll be easier for you to move on because there will be other men you'll be able to pick from.

The majority of women I know (including my clients) who get married were actively looking for a relationship. They were out there! They told their friends, did the online personals, magazine and newspaper personals, went to dances, single events, cruises bars, nightclubs, weddings, took courses. It was like a part time job for them. Women still meet men through life and chance encounters but it takes much longer and is much more sporadic and spaced out. So if getting into a serious relationship is an important goal for you (you're in your thirties and want to have children before the clock starts running out) you should become very proactive about meeting more men and not wait around for Mr. Non-Ambivalent Prince Charming to come galloping up to your apartment door.

There are so many ways to meet men nowadays without having to go to singles bars. I had a client who was very aggressive about meeting new men.

When she broke up with her Ambivalent Man after he strung her along for three years she told everyone she met including her patients (she was a dentist) that she was interested in meeting a new man. Everyone she asked seemed to know someone to introduce her to. In months she was dating three new guys!

Almost every woman I know is meeting men on the personal ad dating sites on the Internet. Even women who can't get out much due to illness, being very consumed with their careers, or taking care of their children at home use it. The process is pretty simple. They meet men through personal ads and then speak to them on the phone. If they feel there's a connection worth exploring they meet with the man in a public place. Don't ever let a man you don't know come to your home! Just go for a coffee date. Meet for a brief amount of time, and if there's no connection, leave. Don't plan to meet for dinner on the first date because you want to be able to leave after a short time if you don't like his company

I can't begin to tell you how many women I know have not only gotten involved in relationships with men they met off these personal ad sites but have married them as well. Don't devalue this process. We're in the computer age. As they say, the future is here! Besides, if you're going on a variety of blind dates you'll be out of the house and not fixating on your Ambivalent Man who's jerking you around.

Stop Chasing Chemistry!

The biggest thing standing in the way of women finding a non-Ambivalent Man is their tenacious commitment to chasing chemistry. Often chemistry is deceptive. Sometimes even the best of us can feel chemistry for a psychopath! Don't be such a chemistry junkie because it can possibly lead you down the wrong path. Get beyond chemistry! Instead of focusing on chemistry, focus on these qualities:

- **He's consistent.** He's not ambivalent; he says one thing and does what he says.
- **He doesn't lie.** Lying is a symptom of a character disorder; a man who lies is untrustworthy, deceptive, and will probably lie to you again and again.
- **He has a job.** Even if it's a crappy job he's a stable person who has the emotional capacity to hold down a job.
- **He asks you questions about yourself.** He's really interested in trying to know you, not just trying to   get immediate gratification.

257

- **He doesn't keep pushing sex.** Although his sexual aggression might make you feel admired and loved, often it's because the guy isn't looking for a relationship.

Stop Drawing Ambivalent Men into Your Life!

Breaking the cycle of dating Ambivalent Men isn't easy, but it's possible. Here are some tips to help you break your habit and avoid getting hurt.

- Get involved only with men who are interested in you. If you see you have to keep pursuing a man, drop him. Don't get attached to a man you have to keep running after.
- If he starts giving you problems in the beginning confront him, and if he does it again, drop him. Don't get attached to a man who is mean, critical, abusive, and argumentative.
- Don't stay so focused on one man, hoping for a commitment. Date more than one man until you find a normal relationship where he's interested, consistent, and committed.

Esther was a very self-assured woman. When she met a man she was interested in she'd go after him without any hesitation. She believed in totally following her heart so when she felt chemistry she'd literally jump right into bed with a man. The only problem was she seemed to get involved only with Ambivalent Men. She decided to change the way she related to men and see what happened. She still allowed herself to make the first move on a guy, but that was it. No more second and third moves. She also stopped having sex with men so quickly. A couple of guys never called her again after she politely turned down their invitations to go back to their apartment after a date. However, a man she met at the beach didn't seem to mind. They became friends before they became sexually involved. She's thrilled that he's not ambivalent and reports that their relationship is becoming very serious.

Make a Commitment to Yourself

Make a commitment not to fall for an Ambivalent Man no matter how difficult it is. When you feel the urgency to be with an Ambivalent Man, turn him down because now you are committed to a different kind of man and a different kind of life. This commitment can't be taken lightly. If you are dating an Ambivalent Man and he's hurting you again and again, you have no one to blame but yourself. You need to work to get what you want and need. Here are some steps to take to change your own Ambivalent Man patterns:

- Become aware of triggers that cause you to automatically run to an Ambivalent Man.
- Change the way you react to your triggers.
- Be in touch with both the vulnerable needy side of you *and* the stronger independent side of you.
- Accept setbacks.
- Be willing to do whatever it takes to stay away from Ambivalent Men.
- Be willing to reach out to your support network when you are feeling vulnerable.
- Keep working on your belief system.

Tell yourself 100 times a day if you have to: "There are other kinds of men out there besides Ambivalent Men. There are men who are not confusing and mixed up. There are men I can be attracted to and develop a relationship with besides Ambivalent Men." Say this statement to yourself as a mantra.

Don't just read the concepts presented in this book—use them actively. Actively take it day to day, minute to minute, second to second. Make the commitment to change.

Change Your Standards

I once had a client who engaged only with impossible Ambivalent Men, complaining that she'd already lowered her standards by dating men who weren't as educated as she was. What she didn't realized was she picked the wrong standard to lower. It doesn't matter how educated or good-looking he is—if he lies to you and is unreliable, you are lowering your standards to be with him. Raise your standards by dating only men whose feelings and behavior remain consistent. In the future, try not to place so much emphasis on his looks or if he can dance. Instead, focus on his character, how he treats you, and if he has the emotional capacity to sustain relationships.

Jill will openly admit that she likes men who have a good "rap." She doesn't like shy men—she likes men who are slick, who have a smooth line. Then she'll complain till the cows come home that she can't find a man of substance! Action speaks louder than words. Some men know just the right words to seduce you by making you feel desired and special. But you don't feel so desired a week later when you never hear from the guy with the great seductive "rap" again! Besides if a man is charming and knows how to engage women in a stimulating dialogue, it's only a skill! That's all it is. So why do you give it so much importance?

Strive for a Normal Relationship

It's normal to feel uncomfortable with change even if it's for the better. If you are used to unreliable, inconsistent, confusing Ambivalent Men, it could take some adjusting to get used to a different kind of man. These are the characteristics of a *normal* relationship:

- The relationship escalates. It doesn't go backward, and it doesn't stay the same. It progresses as you grow closer and form a deeper bond.

- You don't have to call your girlfriends for advice every time you have a date with him or get a voice mail from him.

- You don't have a nervous breakdown every time you have contact with him. It's a relationship, not a   made-for-TV movie.

- The relationship doesn't cause you to feel pain and confusion all the time.

- The relationship adds to your life and energy rather than depleting you.

- The relationship is consistent, safe, and free of chaos.

Bianca had stopped dating for years from being so burnt out from meeting only men who seemed incapable of a healthy long-term relationship. Then, while she was home working on a writing project, she met Sal a computer wiz. He was laid off from his high tech job and working as an electrician, a skill he had learned from his father and which earned his way through college and graduate school. He was assigned to work on Bianca's apartment through the management company of her building. They seemed to have a lot in common and ended up getting into a lengthy conversation while he worked on the wiring in her place. When the job was over, he asked if she wanted to go out some time. When they went to lunch the next week Sheila was surprised at how smoothly things went between them. He was reliable, kind, and considerate. It was a little hard getting use to being with him because she was used to more complicated, high-maintenance men. Basically they had a great time. No games. No aggravation. The more they saw each other, the more anxious she got waiting around for the other shoe to drop. She came to see me, because she was afraid she'd sabotage the relationship to get the dramatic ending over with before he did. Between therapy and her support network she was able to work through her anxiety and they moved in together. He got a great job in a major corporation in the computer field and last I heard they were planning their wedding.

Mourn Your Loss

Often women ask me if I can assure them that if they leave their Ambivalent Man they will find the same great passion with another man. The truth is every relationship with a man is different. Every encounter is unique, like a snowflake. Every man will offer you something more in a different area. No two experiences are ever the same.

There are no guarantees that you will ever feel the unio mystica with another man that you feel with your Ambivalent Man. Part of the reason is that your great passion is fed by the threat of his abandonment and distance. Its hard to feel unio mystica with someone you're with all the time and who is always there for you. You have to choose whether you want to endure all the pain and heartache that often comes with unio mystica. You may experience other pleasurable feelings with another kind of man that your

Ambivalent Man couldn't provide for you, such as consistent love,

permanent partnership, and a future. Unfortunately the passion may not be as

intense. You must accept this truth if you want to stop falling for Ambivalent

Men.

FIFTEEN

LEAVING AND LETTING GO OF AN

AMBIVALENT MAN

When Tina (from Chapter 13) told Brad she didn't want to see him anymore he continued to call her anyway. Finally, she confronted him about his inability to let go. Brad told Tina that he missed her but still wasn't ready to make a commitment. Frustrated and fed up, Tina decided to make a complete break from Brad. She was very firm this time when she told Brad to stop calling. She explained clearly that anything they had between them was over and she was moving on. She never heard from Brad again.

The Last Step Before Leaving an Ambivalent Man

If you have any uncertainties about leaving your Ambivalent Man you should consider having one last discussion or confrontation with him to determine whether or not there's any chance he will change and be better able to meet your needs. This way you will be firm about your decision and will

266

avoid any future obsessing or second-guessing. By confronting your Ambivalent Man, you're clearing the decks. If, after your discussion, you're still not getting what you want and need, walk away with your head held high. You can feel strong in your decision to leave your Ambivalent Man once and for all.

How you handle the situation depends on what type of Ambivalent Man you are dealing with. The following discussion is a very brief summarization of ways you can discuss or confront your Ambivalent Man.

The Runner

You can have this last discussion only when the Runner has returned (never when he's on the run). You can explain that you no longer trust him due to his tendency to abandon you. You can tell him some concrete changes you want him to make in order for you to feel safe enough to continue having a relationship with him.

The Man Who Plays Parlor Games

Don't make yourself more vulnerable to his games! A Man Who Plays Parlor Games is choosing not to have a relationship with you. There's no need to feed his ego by asking about a relationship—you're only opening yourself up to more of his ambivalent behavior. Therefore, try to end your connection to him as best you can without a detailed explanation.

The Casual Dater

Explain that you don't want to casually date anymore. You want a relationship. Tell him that if he can't offer you more than casual dating then you'd prefer to no longer see each other.

The Fling Man

Explain that you want more than just flings. Let him know that if he can't offer you something more substantial than random, intense sexual get-togethers you don't want to see him anymore.

The Eternal Bachelor

If he's dragging his heels about making a commitment, you can give him a choice. Either he makes a commitment or you're going to leave. You just don't want to be in a relationship with him under the present circumstances. He's not meeting your needs and it's just something you don't want to live with anymore.

The Ambivalent Cyber Man

When you're e-mailing or instant messaging let him know that you want to upgrade the communication to speaking on the phone or meeting in person. If you see he's not going to come out from behind the computer screen, let him know that it's curtains for your cyber connection.

Saying Goodbye

Once you decide to end your relationship with your Ambivalent Man you can handle it three different ways, depending on your personality, situation, and relationship:

1. **Tell him the truth.** Be honest and tell him what has been bothering you about the relationship. Explain what needs aren't getting met. Tell him what it is about his behavior that's making you leave.

2. **Be vague.** Don't go into details. Explain to him that the relationship just isn't working anymore for you. If you want, you can make excuses up. For instance, tell him that you've gone

back to your old boyfriend or that you need to make a bigger commitment to your career and will be busier now. Then there's the old reliable: "I need some space right now." Just give him the same vague excuses men tell women all the time! He's been jerking you around for long enough. At this point, you've already told him what's bothering you, and he's still neglecting your needs, so you don't owe him any more explanations.

3. **Avoid him.** If you really hate confrontations, do the fadeout. Make yourself unavailable. Don't answer his phone calls. These tactics are good for a man you don't know that well and don't want to bother with the emotional turmoil of a heavy discussion. It may seem uncaring and insensitive, but sometimes it's the shortest distance to peace of mind. This tactic also works for men who act atrocious and who aren't even worth bothering with anymore.

\

Letting Him Go

After you decide to leave your Ambivalent Man, you'll likely go through some difficult times. Here are some guidelines to make the transition a little easier.

Don't Make a Scene

No matter how you decide to break it off, you don't have to get dramatic about leaving him. You're not a victim. The only things a scene accomplishes are to make you look like you have emotional problems, are very needy, or are a frustrated actress. It's unnecessary. Be strong and firm about your decision. Be grown-up and mature. You're making the best decision for yourself and moving on with your life. There is no need for theatrics.

Stick to Your Decision

No matter how lonely or insecure you get, stick to your decision. If you go back, you will lose all of your credibility with him. Chances are he'll resent your rejecting him and be even less enthusiastic about making changes than he was before. As a result, you'll be even worse off—whatever relationship you have left will be downgraded and not geared toward meeting your needs.

Don't Second-Guess or Obsess about Your Decision

Stick to your guns! Have confidence in your decision and stick with it. Don't start thinking "What if I had done this? What if I had done that? If only this, if only that." Or "I made a gigantic mistake because I'll never meet a man as great as him." These types of thoughts only serve to undo what you've done. It was a hard process to make the break, so stand by your choice. The only point of true power is in the present. So don't look back.

Brenda told Alfred that she didn't want to see him anymore because he didn't want to make a commitment to her. They had been dating a year already and Brenda knew that she was ready to get married and start a family. At first she felt good about her decision, but then she went on a few blind dates and missed Alfred desperately. She couldn't stop second-guessing her decision. She kept thinking about everything that led to her breaking up with him. Finally, unable to contain her regret anymore, she called Alfred and told him that she changed her mind and wanted to see him again. They went out for another two weeks when she started to get frustrated that he wouldn't make a commitment to her and confronted him again. He sounded like a broken record when he told her there was no future. She broke up with him again, upset that she now had to go through the emotional work and pain of missing him a second time.

You Don't Need Closure

This is a biggy. Lots of people go back to the person they broke up to redo the ending because they want to make the closure just right. They usually claim it's because they want it to end things on an upbeat, positive note. Forget how it ends. It's always going to be messy. There's going to be pain and heartache when it's over because it's a loss. The more you keep going back to undo the prior ending the more foolish and desperate you look. And you'll keep having to compulsively repeat it like a vicious cycle. Make up your mind to end it; then let it go and work through all your feelings about your Ambivalent Man by yourself or with people in your support system

Nancy broke up with Chad three months prior to coming to see me. She explained that Chad was always flirting with women. Nancy told him she wouldn't see him anymore unless he proved his love for her by getting engaged. Besides, they had been dating for almost two years and she wanted to either get married or end their relationship, Chad said he wasn't ready to commit so Nancy told him it was over. After thinking about it, Nancy

273

decided she should at least give him an opening, just in case he changed his mind and want to call her. After ruminating about this for days she called Chad to share her thoughts. They got together to talk, but ended up having sex without making any changes in their relationship. The next day Nancy felt enraged and humiliated that she just had a fling with her ex without getting back together. She called him again and told him off for "using me for sex." He got angry, telling her that she wanted it as much as he did. Nancy couldn't stop thinking about what happened for weeks and decided that she wanted to have better closure. After all, they had been great friends as well as lovers and she didn't want things to end on bad terms. She called him, but Chad sounded angry as he picked up the phone. He told her he had a new girlfriend and didn't want Nancy to call anymore. Nancy felt humiliated and devastated, wishing that she had just left things the way they were the first time they broke up

Don't Worry about Giving Back His Things

Don't use the excuse of returning some of his things as a reason to see him again. For instance, if all you have are a couple of his tee shirts, just throw them out, use them yourself, or hide them away in a closet. Give him his things back only if he demands it. If he has some of your things, ask for them only if it's completely necessary. This is important because seeing him can ruin your healing process and that's the last thing you need now. You're better off having no contact until a long time has passed and you are truly over him.

Meredith made a decision to break up with Kirk because he had almost every symptom of an Ambivalent Man. The trait that bothered her most was his unreliability. The problem was, he had the keys to her apartment and her favorite gold necklace, which was a family heirloom. She was scared that if she went over to pick up her things she'd melt in his arms like butter. She decided it was best not to seem him, so she asked him if his friend could drop her keys and necklace off at her job, which Kirk agreed to do.

Shirley was having a hard time forgetting Brian even though she had ended things with him. She asked him to come pick up his things but he never did. He was a grad student and she often helped him study. One night she got tired of crying every time she looked at his political science book that he seemed to have forgotten about. She took the book and threw it in the incinerator in her building. She felt much better so she took all the other things he left in her apartment and threw them out, too. After getting his belongings out of her life, she felt is was easier to keep him out of her thoughts and move on with her life.

Get Ready to Miss Him

Even if he rejected or abused you, you are going to miss him. Even though you actually broke up with him, you're still going to miss him. When you let go of someone you were attached to, it hurts. It's a universal truth for everyone. So you're going to have to endure the feelings and tough it out. You'll have to go through mourning the loss of the relationship and the future you wanted to have with him. Be prepared—this is hard emotional work! Here are the five stages of getting over a loss:

1.   **Denial.** You don't want to face the reality that it's over. You're in emotional shock. You keep replaying moments from the relationship over and over in your mind. You think he's going to call or come back to you.

2.   **Anger.** You feel enraged at him for hurting you, disappointing you, and not coming through for you. You have to fight the urge to bombard him with angry letters, phone calls, and e-mails.

3. **Depression.** You feel depressed about the loss of your Ambivalent Man. You cry a lot. You curl up with your favorite ice cream and watch sappy movies, wallowing in your misery. You sleep more than usual.

4. **Despair.** You feel despair, sadness, and grief. You have trouble seeing the light at the end of the tunnel. You feel as though things are never going to get better.

5. **Acceptance.** You've move through your mourning and accept the loss of your Ambivalent Man. You feel better and stronger about yourself. You're now able to move on.

Go Back to Your Support Group for Encouragement

Don't be afraid to depend on your support system to talk to and process your feelings. Don't stay isolated even though you're mourning. If it gets too hard for you, consider seeking professional help. Seeing a psychotherapist during this period can give you insight as well as support. It can make this experience a time of growth and increasing self-awareness rather than just about sadness and loss.

Support group warning! If anybody in your support network upsets you or makes you more obsessive than you already are, do not include that person in your support network. Go with your instinct.

Doris was having a difficult time forgetting about Steve, an Ambivalent Man she had a brief relationship with. She felt lucky she had a great support system filled with friends and family members. She was having a particularly hard time one Saturday because they usually went out on Saturday nights. She called Georgia, one of her friends, for support and to express her feelings. She was shocked when Georgia told her that Steve was probably with another woman already. Doris felt like a knife went through her. Although it was a possibility that he *was* with someone else, hearing a friend say it so bluntly not only didn't help her in her healing process, but made her want to call him to find out if he was seeing another woman. Doris had wanted only emotional support to get through her day, and instead Georgia had made her feel worse Doris had her hair done and took herself out to lunch to calm herself down and to try and recover from Georgia's insensitive bluntness. She decided that she would never call Georgia for support ever again.

Don't E-Mail or Instant Message That Man!

In this high-tech day and age it is so easy to impulsively contact a man when you're trying to let go of him. So, not only do you have to control yourself from calling your Ambivalent Man, you can't e-mail him or IM him, either. Remember, e-mailing and IM-ing are equivalent to calling him! It's still a way of reaching out, just a different from of technology. So if you're trying to leave an Ambivalent Man, no calling, and no e-mailing or IM-ing allowed!

Take Him off Your Buddy List

If you frequently corresponded with your Ambivalent Men online, take him off your buddy list. When you see his name flashing on your buddy list you may have a hard time resisting chatting with him online, or e-mailing him or calling him on the phone.

Cyndi had been involved with Ivan who was separated from his wife. When Cyndi realized that Ivan was never going to get a divorce she decided to end things. Unfortunately a lot of their correspondence had been over the computer, e-mailing and instant messaging each other all day. Although she explained why she left him, Ivan kept IM-ing her during the day just to say hello. Cyndi found it hard to resist his contacts and would often respond to his instant messages. When she told me she had him on her buddy list, I told her to remove his name so she wouldn't even know he was online. Cyndi explained it was easier for her to know he was online so she could prepare for his instant messages rather than be surprised by them. Although this was totally logical I still felt that not seeing his name would make it easier to let go of him. I also suggested that she not answer his instant messages or e-mails.

Don't Stay Friends with Him (At Least for This Year)

Why would you be buddies with him anyway? Did you really have that much in common that you really need his friendship? Did you have a business together? Are you partners in the same career as Sonny and Cher?

Staying friends with him is just an excuse to be in contact with him. You're really hoping that if you stay friends with him he'll miraculously change and become unambivalent.

Unfortunately, you're just deluding yourself. Don't fall into this trap. Not only will staying friends keep you from letting go of him and moving on, it will give him an opening to keep acting ambivalent, confusing you, and creating chaos in your life. Keep in mind that this relationship was about sex, chemistry, and romance. This was not a friendship or else you wouldn't be reading this book. So stop playing mind games with yourself. Let go of the denial. Own your true feelings for him even if things didn't work out.

Ruth decided to end things with Melvin because he just wasn't boyfriend material. He'd come and go as he pleased, calling her last minute when he wanted to get together. Fed up with his inability to go any further with the relationship, Ruth told him she was dating other men and didn't think they should see each other anymore. Melvin said he understood but wanted to stay friends. Ruth agreed to giving being "just friends" a chance. Melvin continued to casually drop by and before she knew it things were right back to where they started. Since they were now officially friends he even told her about other women he also saw occasionally, which Ruth found unbearable to listen to. After getting support from the women in my support group she finally decided to cut all her ties to Melvin and no longer stay friends with him. Although she still misses Melvin and wonders how he's doing, she feels she's made a lot of progress in letting go and moving on.

Do Not Seek Revenge

Do not seek retaliation in any way. Revenge is just another way to stay attached to him. Work out your anger with a therapist or people in your support network. Taking revenge also makes you look desperate and emotionally disturbed. Vengeful behavior only makes a man thank his lucky stars that he's not involved with you anymore, rather than miss you or feel regretful. Think of your pride and integrity.

Erica was angry that Curtis had a sexual fling with her but didn't want a relationship. Her friends suggested she stop spending so much times being angry at Curtis and use that energy to find a new man. However, Erica couldn't stop thinking about how tricked she felt and wanted to teach him a lesson. Consumed with thoughts of revenge, she started calling people they knew mutually to tell them what a user he is and that they should warn other women to stay away from him. Still not satisfied, Erica eventually called his boss and made up complaints about him to try to get him fired. She came to see me when Curtis slammed her with a lawsuit for slander.

What to Do When You Need to Contact Him

If you have to be in touch with him due to children or business matters, just speak about what's necessary, and that's it. Don't initiate small talk. Don't flirt. Discuss only what's necessary. Set firm boundaries in the contact that you do have. Do not discuss your personal issues with him, and do not ask him about his personal life.

Diane split up with Tomas to whom she was married for six years They had two children they both cherished. Although Diane had the strength not to call Tomas, she had to stay in touch with him for their children. She decided to speak to him only about the children when he called or when she absolutely had to talk to him about them. She never spoke to him about her personal life unless it somehow involved their children. She would not ask him about his life. No chitchat when she saw him. It was only about the kids. Although this took some self-discipline she found that keeping boundaries with him helped her tremendously.

What If He Keeps Coming Back?

Unless he's willing to change, tell him firmly that it's over and he must leave you alone. Sometimes Ambivalent Men continue to act ambivalent by continuing to stay in touch you even though they still don't want to commit, give you more, change, or give up other women. It's important to keep in mind that all of his pursuing when you're no longer interested doesn't mean he's going to change. It's just an Ambivalent Man acting out his ambivalence.

When your Ambivalent Man continues to contact you after you've told him not to, he is not honoring your boundaries or taking you seriously. If you tell a man to stop calling you and mean business, he will most likely stay away. If he still doesn't leave you alone just hang up the phone or even change your phone number. If this doesn't work, then he's harassing you and it has to become a legal matter. However, this usually doesn't happen with Ambivalent Men. Once they know a woman isn't interested and doesn't want to play anymore, they usually go away.

Renee was friends with Pierre for a little while before they became sexually involved. When Renee realized that Pierre was still dating other women while they were now romantically entwined, she confronted him. He told her that he wasn't ready to be with just one woman now. Renee explained that she was looking for a serious boyfriend and thought it was best for her if they no longer dated each other. Pierre said he understood but called her a month later just to chat. Renee talked to him for a few minutes but again told him it would be the last time they spoke. Ignoring her boundary, he continued to leave her messages. Renee asked him if she were so important to him why did he want to date other women when they had been seeing each other? Pierre told her that he couldn't see them having a future together as a couple but wanted to be friends anyway. Insulted that Pierre wanted only friendship and not a long-term romantic relationship, she firmly told him to stop calling her. Even after being told off, Pierre still called one more time. When Renee heard his voice she hung up the phone. She felt bad being rude, but telling him politely not to call was pointless since he didn't listen. Hanging up on him seemed to be the only way to get rid of him once and for all! Pierre finally stopped calling Renee.

What to Do If You Have a Strong Urge to Contact Him

When your relationship with your Ambivalent Man is over, it can be difficult to fight the tendency to want to stay in contact with him. Before you contact him, take a deep breath and read the guidelines below.

- Make yourself wait before contacting him. You may change your mind if you wait at least a couple of hours or even a day.
- Distract yourself by doing something you love.
- Stay busy. Make plans with friends, go on a trip, do whatever you can to keep yourself active so you don't think about calling him.
- Work on your career.
- Call someone in your support system.
- Call a brand-new man.

- Make a list of the terrible things he's done that hurt and disappointed you.

- Get away from whatever is triggering you to think of him.

- Go out to a party or social event where you can meet new people.

- Learn to go out alone. Buy yourself lunch, see a movie, see a play. By going out on your own, you'll learn that you don't have to depend on others.

What to Do If You Have a Setback

If you have a setback, just forgive yourself for taking a couple of steps backward and start all over again. Don't pity yourself or beat yourself up. Remember, progress is often three steps forward and one step back. It's rarely a straight line.

Daphne had worked with Jack for over a year. Although they had separate offices he always came into her office to chat, often in a flirtatious manner, giving her the impression that he wanted to date her. One evening they were out together at a work function and Daphne confronted Jack about his seductive conversations (some of them were sexualized) in her office. He said that he was just bored at their job and that's why he came to her office. He even owned up to being seductive but claimed he wasn't really interested in anything happening between them. Deciding that Jack was definitely an Ambivalent Man Who Plays Parlor Games, Daphne decided that she wouldn't let Jack come into her office anymore and started keeping her door closed. One week she had an argument with her supervisor and was having a hard time concentrating at work. Wanting not to think about her boss, she completely forgot about her problem with Jack and accidentally left her door open. Jack started coming around again and flirting with her. Daphne knew she had a setback by letting him back into her life with his nasty Parlor Games. The next time he came into her office, gazing into her eyes with his flirtatious grin, she told Jack that she really had a lot of work to do and to stop spending his time in her office when he needed a break. No matter how upset she was, Daphne kept her door closed until Jack got the hint and stopped coming around for good.

Selma had a casual dating relationship with Mitchell who was a bona fide Fling Man. She was having a good time until she realized that she was developing deep feelings for him. When she finally saw that it was never going to be more than sporadic flings with Mitchell, she broke up with him. Selma went out with a few different men but was always disappointed that she didn't have that great chemistry she experienced with Mitchell. One night she was PMSing and feeling especially lonely, so she called Mitchell. He was only too happy to hear from her and invited himself over. They had a night of passionate lovemaking and then he left the next morning. Just as in the past, she didn't hear from him for awhile. Feeling abandoned, she was angry at herself for having a major setback. She knew she had to pick herself up and start all over. She worked on building up her sense of self and didn't contact Mitchell. When he got around to finally calling her, she told him she had a good time the last time they were together but realized it was a mistake and didn't think they should see each other again. Although there were times that Selma still missed Mitchell, she was determined not to have another setback, which helped her to have the strength not to call him anymore.

Making a decision to leave is difficult enough, but really letting go and moving on is excruciatingly hard work. I once heard someone say that breaking up with someone is like childbirth. If everyone remembered how much pain they were in the last time they broke up with someone they no one would ever fall in love again.

Unfortunately, breaking up is a necessary process if the relationship you're in is not healthy. The good thing is that once you've moved through the process of leaving and letting go, you will be open and available to a

healthier, more successful life and relationships.

SIXTEEN

THE AMBIVALENT WOMAN

Tricia, a woman in her late twenties, came to see me because she was having a hard time staying in an ongoing relationship with one man. She reported having had more than twenty romantic relationships since she started college at eighteen. She felt bad that she was usually attracted to men who had no intention of making a commitment.

Tricia had a career in the arts that she enjoyed tremendously. She had an active social life and was close to her family and friends. Upon closer examination of her life, she realized that when she was involved with men who were interested in a permanent relationship she usually felt closed in. But then she'd feel disappointed and lonely when the kind of man she was drawn to couldn't love her the way she wanted. One evening she came to her session right after a date with a man she felt totally confused about, and announced that she was fed up with working on her romantic conflicts and announced that the problem was that she was an Ambivalent Woman.

The Ambivalent Woman Quiz

Can you identify with Tricia's dilemma? Are you an Ambivalent woman? Let's find out.

1. Do you have a long history of involvements with Ambivalent Men?

2. Do you have any history of abandonment or abuse as a child or teenager?

3. Is it more natural for you to date a man who's sexy but noncommittal, than one who wants marriage but is less exciting?

4. Have you struggled for more than three years with the conflict of wanting a man who can commit and then not being attracted to him?

5. Have you rejected dating or having a relationship with a man who appeared seriously interested in you? More than two times?

6. Have you gotten caught up within the last two years in at least two entanglements with any of the five prototypes of Ambivalent Men I've described?

7. Do any of my descriptions of Ambivalent Men remind you of yourself?

8. Are you ambivalent in other parts of your life (therapy, work, girlfriends)

9. Do you have a hard time with commitment?

10. Is being married or having a life with a significant other not an important goal for you?

If you answered yes to at least three questions there's a good possibility that you are an Ambivalent Woman.

What's an Ambivalent Woman?

An Ambivalent Woman has conflicted feelings about her relationships with men. She claims to long for a committed, long-term relationship or marriage, yet she primarily gets involved with men who make it very clear in their words and behavior that they don't want commitment. An Ambivalent Woman completely blames men for her marriage-less state, because she's not in touch with the parts of herself that doesn't want to be in a relationship. She projects her own issues onto men, blaming them so she doesn't have to take responsibility for the parts of herself that doesn't want a long-term relationship or marriage.

These are some of the reason why a woman is ambivalent:

- She's afraid of pregnancy.

- She's burnt out from having been disappointed so many times.

- She doesn't want to take the chance of being been hurt again (having been hurt many times in past love relationships).

- She has a general fear of rejection.

- She doesn't want to put the energy or time into relationships due to her career or other interests that are taking up much of her time and interest (including raising children on her own).

- She feels she doesn't have the physical attractiveness to compete with all the other women who are trying to find men.

- She has not worked through her issues about her father or her mother (hasn't emotionally separated from one or both of them).

- She's afraid of closeness.

- She was sexually abused as a child.

How to Work Through Your Ambivalence

Although this is not a simple answer, I can tell you to at least get in touch with the parts of you that don't want a long-term relationship. I know that after years of dating, aborted relationships, and disappointment it's easy to get defensive and emotionally close down. However, in order to eventually love again you have to be open and vulnerable. It's part of the process of falling in love. The only way to do this is to work through any of the residual feelings you still have about men who've let you down, disappointed, hurt, or betrayed you. If you're in touch with all the different parts of your self, including your anger and aggression, then you won't sabotage a possibly healthy relationship.

For instance, Tricia realized that when she met men who appeared very interested in her and available she could sometimes be defensive and unavailable by waiting a few days to return their phone calls or turning down dates with them. Although she claimed to want a relationship very badly, she was unaware she was distancing until we discussed it in one of her sessions. When she became aware of her own

294

anger at men and was able to express it in her therapy session and with her friends, she no longer sabotaged possible relationships and began choosing emotionally available men.

Writing Exercises

Here are some writing exercises to help you get in touch with your own feelings of ambivalence about wanting to have a relationship with a man. After you answer the questions, process your feelings with someone in your support network or with a therapist. Look at the following questions and write down your experiences and feelings:

- Describe the disappointments you've had with men since you've been dating. Describe the times you've been rejected, the times you've been lied to, the times men have betrayed you, and the times men have broken up with you.

- Describe what it's like to be with a man who's completely emotionally available and in love with you, but who's not terrifically exciting. Imagine being with this man for many years filled with emotional security from his devotion. What does that feel like to you?

- Project into the future. What does it feel like to lead a long complete life and never be committed to one man? Lonely? Exciting? Independent? Free? Sad?

- Has anything happened in your childhood that causes you to feel anxiety when you get very close to a man? What feelings are coming up for you?

- Describe times in your life when you turned down opportunities to have encounters or relationship with men who were ambivalent. What did that feel like when you rejected their offers? Did it feel powerful? Did you feel a sense of loss of an opportunity?

- Describe times in your life when you turned down a man who was not exciting, stimulating, or appealing to you although he was very much into you. Did you feel a sense of relief? Did you feel a sense of loss? Did you feel frustrated? Did you feel angry?

The more aware you are of all your feelings the less you will disassociate from them. Disassociating from your feelings causes you to act them out, just as the Ambivalent Men I've describe in this book do. Your self-awareness of your own resistance to what you claim you want will help you in the already difficult process of finding a healthy and satisfactory love relationship.

SEVENTEEN

HEALTHY RELATIONSHIPS: MEN WHO WANT DEEP PERSONAL INVOLVEMENT

After you've grieved and moved on from the Ambivalent Man who's not available to give you what you need or want, perhaps you're ready to consider a man who may have more capacity for a healthy long-term relationship. I refer to this type of man as one who wants Deep Personal Involvement, or DPI, with a woman. A man who is capable of DPI is not out to play games. He's not looking for a trophy wife or wanting to act out his childhood anger and frustration that he hasn't yet resolved. He wants intimacy and emotional connection in a deep way just as you do.

How do you know you've met a man who is capable of DPI? These are the signs to look for:

- He doesn't act ambivalent.

- He makes you feel secure.

- He's predictable.

- He's not always "on the make."

- He talks and acts with consistency.

- His feelings about you stay the same (they've don't waver like the stock market).

- He wants to go out on normal dates.

- He wants a relationship.

- He wants to be part of a couple.

- He wants to get married.

- He looks beyond your appearance.

- He doesn't make you feel as if you're going crazy.

- He adds to your life rather than depletes from it.

- He's dependable.

- He's supportive.

- He's easy to understand.

- He doesn't lie.

- He's not an enigma.

- He earns his own money—legally.

- He has a job.

- He's working on his future.

- You know where you stand with him.

How to Hook Up with a DPI Man

There are no particular places to meet DPI men. You just have to keep your eyes and ears always open. The unfortunate spin to this is that because they do want relationships, men who want DPI are often in a relationship already. It may sound strange, but be on the lookout for men friends or acquaintances who are ending relationships and marriages with their girlfriends or wives. Not everyone who goes through a divorce or breakup has severe psychological problems. Often people just outgrow each other, or their needs change, or their careers call for them to leave. So don't be scared of a man who just left a relationship or was left. Although they are vulnerable and can potentially rebound, they are also available.

Emotionally healthy men are a hot commodity, so you've got to be aggressive and on top of things.

Sometimes you can meet them through an introduction from a mutual friend or coworker. Sometimes they'll use the personals just as anyone else, but they're out there and often seriously looking, just like you are. Here are some suggestions for trying to snag a man who wants DPI with a woman.

Don't Waste Time

When you meet a man who's not looking for DPI, cut and run! Cross him off the list no matter how charismatic, handsome, fun, or rich he is. I can't stress this point enough. I meet so many women who waste years on men who frustrate them and deprive them of their desire for long-term, enduring love and commitment. Don't let yourself fall into this trap anymore. Cut your losses and *move on;* don't stay fixated on him. Instead, leave yourself open and available both physically and emotionally to men who want DPI with a woman. Women who are successful in finding permanent love invest time only in men who can help them achieve their goal. When they see it's not going anywhere, they're out of there so fast they leave skid marks. They don't keep dragging out a drama that leads only to pain and heartache.

Make the First Move

If you're lucky enough to meet a man who wants DPI and is available, then make the first move. Unlike the Ambivalent Man, with this guy it's okay to initiate, at least in the beginning. Don't be passive. Don't wait around like a flower waiting to get picked. However, if you make the first and even the second move, that's it! Afterward, it's up to him. You've slammed the ball into his court so now it's his turn to slam it back into yours.

Keep Working on Your Issues

Don't let your own psychological issues lower your chances of developing a successful relationship with a man who actually has the capacity for DPI. Work on your own emotional baggage. If you have leftover problems about your father, work on them. If you have issues about control or jealousy, go for help. Talk to people in your support system, get counseling, go to workshops, read books. Make sure you're not standing in the way of getting what you want. The odds are already tough enough. Finding romantic love is a stressful situation, so the healthier you are emotionally, the higher your chances of success will be because you'll be able to withstand all the trials and tribulations you may have to endure to achieve your goal. Don't sabotage your chances for success! Keep working on your emotional health

Don't Expect Perfection

Even though he may not have severe character problems, he's still human and capable of disappointing you. Here are two things to be aware of:

1.   **He's going to have baggage.** Anybody who's been single or around the block a few times has probably been hurt, so he's going to have baggage. Even if he truly wants a relationship and appears capable of one, there's still the chance that his defensiveness from past relationships and/or marriages can take its toll and cause him to bolt. So in the beginning you still have to be careful. There are no guarantees, no matter how normal he appears.

2.   **He may be scared.** It's a whole new world for men and women. Our roles keep changing. Women today are much more emotionally demanding than our mothers and grandmothers were. Emotionally we want more from men now than ever before. It's not the old days when women's roles were laid out for them—they married a man who took care of them financially while they stayed home and took care of the children. Today, men are anxious in their new roles, even the men who are psychologically healthy.

Don't Think Self-Destructive Thoughts

When a man who wants DPI disappoints you in any way, don't immediately start thinking awful things about yourself. Don't attack yourself the second a man in any way rejects you. Remember, his problem has nothing to do with you, so stop blaming it on your looks, height, weight, teeth, clothes, how much money you make, job, career, or children. The list is endless, and you could torture yourself forever. This type of thinking is not only self-destructive, it's downright masochistic. Say this twenty times a day if you have to:

Don't personalize everything. *It's not always about you.*

You must do whatever it takes not to attack yourself. It's hard enough being out there and trying to find a healthy loving relationship. You don't need to make things worse by driving yourself crazy. Instead, nurture yourself. You need to emotionally restore yourself. Do whatever it takes to let go of this depleting incident and move on in the relationship or another man. Just don't take it out on yourself.

You Will Feel Anxiety in the Beginning of a New Relationship

No matter how normal a guy is, there is always anxiety and stress in the beginning of any relationship. This is because you don't know what's going to happen. He's an unknown entity. You're scared of being vulnerable. So don't think it's just you. Just accept the initial anxiety and go with the flow. Reach out to the people in your support system to express your feelings to and work through your anxiety. You need them to give you a reality check now and then. When a problem arises, ask for their objective opinions on how much of it is your issues and how much of it is his. Be grateful for the people in your support network and don't forget to thank them for being there for you.

Keep Your Eye on the Ball

You need to keep exploring what it is that turns you on about a man. If you still see that you are attracted to hopeless Ambivalent Men for reasons that are emotionally unhealthy, then you need to keep working on yourself. Go to workshops, therapy, read, and speak with other women. Dig deep to discover where your attraction comes from and use your support system to keep processing these thoughts and ideas

If you want a long-lasting relationship with a man who wants DPI and your exciting but psycho ex-Ambivalent Man comes around, resist the urge to see him, no matter how tempting it is. Think of long-term gratification as opposed to short-term gratification. Work on not being impulsive. Try to be more mature and think of the future—plan for tomorrow instead of today, because the Ambivalent Man won't be there for your tomorrow. Keep your eye on the ball.

EIGHTEEN

CHOICES

Making choices about the kind of man you want to be with has a lot to do with your priorities. Carefully evaluate what you want. Would you rather have a stable, enduring relationship or the thrills and chills of an exciting Ambivalent Man who's just beyond your reach? How do you feel about committing to a man who wants DPI, but is not as stimulating as your ex-Ambivalent Man? Would you describe being with a man who's considerate and kind but not exciting, as "settling"? What does the term "settling" mean to you? Throwing in the towel? Staying with a man you're not to crazy about?

Some women want to get married and start a family. They feel they don't have the time and patience to keep searching for a man who'll give them that special chemistry they've been waiting for. Often they're under pressure from their families, friends, careers. If they finally meet a man they like who's capable of a long-term commitment, who wants to marry them, that's more than enough to set the wedding date. Are these women settling?

To "Settle" Makes Sense

Marcy was twenty-seven and wanted to get married in the worst way. She felt as if her entire family were descendents from the Bible story of Noah's ark because everyone was part of a couple. Weddings were as consistent a social event in her family as Christmas holidays. She had been dating George for as long as she could remember. When she turned twenty-eight she told George they either had to get married or she was going to break up with him. She couldn't believe it when George announced that he thought he might be gay. After she recovered from learning there would never be a future for them, they parted as friends.

Marcy aggressively started searching for a man she considered to be "husband material." She told everyone she knew that she wanted to meet someone. A few of her friends and business colleagues hooked her up with available men they knew. She also did the personals ads and joined a dating service. Marcy was a woman on a mission. If a man had no intentions of wanting to marry in the near future she crossed him off the list and quickly moved on. She eventually narrowed down her suitors to two men: Chris and

Larry. She adored Chris. He was handsome, successful, and fun to be with. Larry, however, was not as attractive, very shy, but had a good job and was a hard worker. He was also very reliable and kind.

When her best friend got engaged, she realized she was the only one from the group of friends she grew up with who was still unattached. Then her younger sister Ali gave birth to her niece. Marcy felt as though she couldn't bear being single and dating for one more moment. That weekend Larry asked Marcy to marry him. Marcy was very happy for the proposal but was concerned that although she liked Larry she knew she wasn't in love with him.

She did feel very attracted to Chris, though. She decided to go on one last date with Chris. Eating dessert following a wonderful dinner at a glamorous French restaurant, Marcy asked Chris his thoughts about the future. He told her that he didn't see himself getting married for a long time. He explained that he enjoyed his independence and didn't even know if he wanted to have kids. Alone in her bedroom that evening Marcy decided that she didn't want to date anymore and wanted to start a new life with a husband, family, white picket fence, and all the trimmings. The next morning she called Larry and told him she'd be happy to marry him.

Do you think that Marcy "settled"?

Compromise Is Good

Almost every married woman I speak to feels that she compromised in some way when she married her husband. I've never spoken to a married women who felt that her husband had every quality she was looking for in a man.

Lynn is a social worker who finally met a man who had every quality she was looking for except that he was not generous with money. From their first date he'd always split everything with her 50-50. He never wanted to pay for dinner, always expecting her to chip in. This was not a trait she liked but felt he had other great qualities that she had been looking for in a potential mate. They're married today and they're still splitting everything right down the middle.

So expect there to be some sort of *compromise* when you commit. For instance, maybe he'll have the look but not the intelligence you imagined a man you'd end up with would have. Or maybe he'll have the success but not the stimulating conversational skills and the ability to relate you'd like him to have. By having certain expectations about the "perfect" man, you are limiting the possibilities. Rather than trying to control every aspect of the perfect man, just relax and let it happen.

Ellen a successful psychologist was very attracted to artistic and bohemian men. However, she preferred spending her free time curled up with a really good book rather than going out looking for men in clubs or doing the personals. After two dateless years she ran into Ted at a gallery opening. Although Ellen was shy, Ted took an interest in her and they went out for coffee that very night. She was disappointed to learn that he had only marginal jobs and didn't appear too ambitious despite his artistic talent. He was also much less educated than she was. She had a doctorate and he had finished only one year of college. However, despite his lack of degrees, he was streetwise and naturally very bright. He also paid a great deal of attention to Ellen and was a wonderful companion. Although she always thought she'd end up with a man who was professional with the same amount of success in her field of study, she decided to marry Ted. He met all of her emotional needs and made her happy.

The Deal Breaker

There may be some qualities that you just wont be able to negotiate on. As they say in *Sex and the City* what is your "deal breaker"? What are the qualities or things about a man that you find intolerable? Something you cannot live with under any circumstances? What trait or behavior would make you prefer to stay single until you draw in your last breath rather than accept? For Marcy, she would not be with a man who was unreliable. Ellen couldn't tolerate a man who was a womanizer. She tended to become in involved with men who were loners like herself.

List five qualities that are your deal breaker:

1.

2.

3.

4.

5.

What Do You Want?

To determine what kind of man you'd like to be with, it's important to determine what you want from life. What are your values? What is important to you? Marcy and Ellen were fortunate that they knew what they wanted.

Marcy wanted marriage above everything else. It was crystal clear to her.

Ellen enjoyed having a calm life. She preferred being by herself than the

stress and chaos of a man who would disrupt her peaceful life she had created

despite her occasional loneliness. She turned down opportunities to be with

other men who were high-maintenance and had problems. She felt relaxed

and at home with Ted, which was exactly what she was looking for.

Set Your Priorities

If marriage and a family is a priority for you, as it was for Marcy, then

you need to focus more on avoiding Ambivalent Men who are terrified of

commitment. You need to be with men who share your goals and priorities of

wanting marriage in their near future.

If incredible passion and unbelievable chemistry is completely

essential, then you may have to give up marriage and raise children without a husband. You just may not be able to get both things in one relationship. That was the decision that Vicki had to make.

Vicki was an attractive forty-year-old actress. Although she never made it to Hollywood stardom, she always managed to support herself with acting jobs in commercials and occasional minor roles and major studio productions. She had been dating Stan for three years when she came to my office. He surprised Vicki when he asked her if she wanted to get married. He said that he wanted to move out of the city in the next few months. He was a carpenter by trade and had visions of buying property and building his own house by hand. Although she liked Stan tremendously she could not decide what to do. She came to see me to help her work through this decision. She worked in therapy on some of her psychological issues about her relationship with her father, who she felt was very distant and aloof. She thought by resolving her past she would feel more sure about what to do with her relationship with Stan.

During our work together she met another man who she felt tremendously attracted to and started to date. She also got cast in a soap opera in Los Angeles. She realized that although she did love Stan she also enjoyed her freedom to date other men freely whenever she felt like it. Vicki also liked that she could pick up and go wherever she wanted, whenever her career called for her to relocate or travel, without having to answer to anyone. Vicki told Stan that even though she loved him she didn't want to get married. She decided that she didn't want to commit herself to one man.

As we can learn by Vicki's story, not all women are looking for marriage and commitment. Once Vicki became more aware of her values and priorities she was not concerned if a man was ambivalent and just decided to enjoy whatever experiences with men came her way.

Can you relate to either Marcy or Vicki? Try the following writing exercises to help you work through your own ideas about what you want.

Your Views on Marriage

Write down your feelings, thoughts, and opinions about what marriage means to you.

- How important is it for you to get married?
- Has marriage been your lifelong dream since you were a girl or teenager?
- Could you live without ever marrying and still feel you had a rich, full life?

- Do you feel envious of girlfriends and family members who are married?

- Are most of the people in your family married? Do you get treated like a second-class citizen if you're single in your family?

- Would you feel as if you're alone or missing out on something if you don't marry?

- What would it be like to have lovers in your life but never marry or live with anyone?

Your Views on Having Children

Write down your feelings, thoughts, and opinions about what having children means to you.

- How important is it for you to have children?

- Could you imagine having children without a husband? Could you be a single mom?

- Is having children an important value for your family you grew up in?

- Would you disappoint your parents if you didn't have children?

- Do you presently have children (other than yours) in your life (nieces, nephews, children of friends)?

- Would you feel deprived or that you're missing out on something if you don't have children?

Your Views on Your Career

Write down your feelings, thoughts, and opinions about what your career means to you.

- How important is your career to you?

- Would marriage and family interfere with your career ambitions?

- Would the amount of time you put into your career interfere with raising children if you decide to have them?

- Would you be willing to give up your career if you were to hook up with a man who wanted to marry but needed to relocate?

- Do you have a flexible career that allows you to devote time to a relationship or family and still have your career?

- Would you prefer to continue putting in most of your energy into your career to guarantee your ongoing success and achievements?

Your Views on Maintaining Your Lifestyle

Write down your feelings, thoughts, and opinions about what your present lifestyle means to you.

- Do you enjoy being alone?

- Do you spend a lot of time alone?

- Would you be happy if you had a lover or lovers without marriage or a live-in arrangement?

- Do you have hobbies and passions that you spend a lot of time with (going to conferences, taking classes, traveling, dancing, writing)?

- Could you compromise on your hobbies and passions if your were to be in a committed relationship or marriage?

- What is your financial situation? Do you sometimes believe it would be easier to live with a partner?

- Would living with a man ruin your independent single life that you've built?

- Do you feel as if you'd be subordinating yourself to a man at this point if you were to live with or marry a man?

Any choice you make will have consequences. If you want constant excitement, thrills, and chills, you can't complain when you see your best friend living a more boring life but with a husband. And vice versa. If you're with a husband who's there for you but isn't someone you're wildly in love with, don't complain when you see your single girlfriend raving about an exciting man she just met! If you love being a free agent, there may be times when something traumatizing happens that you would do anything to have a life partner to rely on. If you love being married there may be times you're so exasperated with your husband you'd do anything to go back in time and have never met him. There's always a yin and a yang, the polarity of opposites.

The Choice Is *Yours*

There is no right or wrong choice for what a women wants when it comes to men and love. Although this may seem like a disappointing statement at first, in a way it's a great one because you are lucky you have so many choices. Only a minute ago in the vast time of civilization, women were forced to marry men they hardly knew or even disliked. Things are also different from the way things were in our mother's and our grandmother's generations. We don't need men to financially support us anymore. We don't even need them to have babies (we can get artificially inseminated). We don't need men to survive. A lot of us have our own work now, our own careers. Some of us make more money than men and are more successful.

Many self-help authors out there proclaim that if you read their books you will be able to magically get married. Their books promote getting married as the grand prize, the Holy Grail. That's not the point of this book. Getting married doesn't mean that you've won. Even in today's progressive culture, marriage is overidealized. Just look at the statistics: 60 percent of marriages end in divorce. Single women live longer than married women. Even though many of the women's stories in this book are about wanting to get married or find a committed relationship, you should know that just as many married women come to me saying how miserable they are in their marriages and wish they were single again.

If you work through your issues from your past the best you can, if you build a life that has meaning, that gives you fulfillment and truth, then you have made it. You have won the prize. Being alone and fulfilled is a choice. There may even be times when a relationship with a man feels intrusive and draining—especially if your life is already stimulating and full with a career, passion about life, and love for friends and family.

The choices you make about the men you allow into your life should be completely up to you. It's not about what your mother, therapist, girlfriends, or even self-help authors think. Your choices should reflect your truth about what you believe and feel. If marriage is primarily what you want then go for it. If remaining single until you meet the man you believe is your soul mate, even if it takes a lifetime, then, as they say "you go, girl."

Whatever choices you make, the most important thing to remember from reading this book is that you must think highly of yourself. You will no longer tolerate destructive acting-out behavior from Ambivalent Men in the service of passion, great sex, or even marriage. As a woman posted on my message board:

If a man stands you up, it is up to you whether to give him another chance. If you keep giving more and more chances then you are condoning his ambivalent acting-out behavior. You are not causing his behavior, just allowing it to persist. All of that being said, there is a huge psychic price to pay for allowing someone to mistreat you. I did it for several months this past year and what devastates me is not that this particular man mistreated me but that I allowed it to continue for so much longer than I needed to. If I had cut it off the first or second or fifth clear sign of there being something amiss, I would have about thirty less "wrongs" to remember and brood over. My healing would have begun in November instead of January.

You don't have to decide right now or tomorrow whether your want to give up your Ambivalent Man, find a new man who wants Deep Personal Involvement, or be by yourself for awhile. You can keep working on your choices because you are a work in progress. None of your decisions are engraved in stone. One great thing about life is that it's a process, and each day holds the possibilities for new chances and unexplored opportunities.

ABOUT THE AUTHOR

Rhonda Findling is the author of *Don't Call That Man! A Survival Guide to Letting Go, Don't Text That Man! A Guide To Self Protective Dating in the Age of Technology, Men Who Run From Love: A Guide To Having A Relationship With A Relationship Phobic Man, Don't Lose That Man! How Women Sabotage Their Opportunities For Successful Romantic Relationships and What They Can Do To Change, Portrait of My Desire, A Teenager's Memoir*, the Don't Text That Man app and The Help Me Rhonda Show short/doc.

Rhonda is a psychotherapist with an international private practice based out of New York. She can be contacted through her website at www.RhondaFindling.com

CPSIA information can be obtained
at www.ICGtesting.com
Printed in the USA
FSOW03n2049120118
43391FS